Understanding Housing Finance

ONE WEEK LOAN

One of the b
financial prin
omy. By taki
Housing Fina
requiring det

The book e
and governm
the advantag
intervene. Th
examples of l
control, hous

This is a ke
both undergra
its relevance i
for those stu
countries.

Peter King is
Housing Rese
Private Dwell

Understanding Housing Finance

Meeting needs and making choices

Second edition

Peter King

Routledge
Taylor & Francis Group

LONDON AND NEW YORK

Second edition published 2009
by Routledge
2 Park Square, Milton Park, Abingdon, Oxon OX14 4RN

Simultaneously published in the USA and Canada
by Routledge
270 Madison Avenue, New York, NY 10016, USA

Routledge is an imprint of the Taylor & Francis Group, an informa business

© 2009 Peter King

Typeset in Sabon and Swis721 by
Florence Production Ltd, Stoodleigh, Devon
Printed and bound in Great Britain by
CPI Antony Rowe, Chippenham, Wilts

British Library Cataloguing in Publication Data
A catalogue record for this book is available from the British Library

Library of Congress Cataloging in Publication Data
King, Peter, 1960–
  Understanding housing finance : meeting needs and making choices/
  Peter King. – 2nd ed.
    p. cm.
  Includes bibliographical references and index.
  1. Housing – Finance – Government policy – Great Britain.
  2. Housing subsidies – Great Britain.   3. Housing authorities –
  Great Britain.   4. Housing policy – Great Britain.   I. Title.
  HD7333.A4K56 2009
  363.5′820941—dc22   2008034308

ISBN10: 0–415–43294–4 (hbk)
ISBN10: 0–415–43295–2 (pbk)
ISBN10: 0–203–88271–7 (ebk)

ISBN13: 978–0–415–43294–8 (hbk)
ISBN13: 978–0–415–43295–5 (pbk)
ISBN13: 978–0–203–88271–9 (ebk)

*In memory of
Thomas Reed Hakin
(1920–2008)*

Contents

Tables

Preface

In the preface to the first edition of this book I made great play of the fact that the book was very much about housing finance without numbers. When I told a colleague that I was doing a second edition, he asked me, 'What's this going to be like? Is it housing finance without the finance?'

'That's exactly right!' I responded, 'How did you guess?' And indeed that was what I intended. In reality, of course, I did not really intend to discuss another topic, but rather I wanted to consider housing finance in a different manner. I wanted to present a conceptual framework – very much a development out of the first edition, at least in its character and ambition – that an intelligent reader (and all people reading this are certainly that) could apply to any particular housing finance policy.

In this edition, therefore, I am taking much more seriously the title, and in particular the word 'understanding'. I want to understand how housing finance systems work *in general*. I want to consider what it takes to understand a financial mechanism in its proper context. For me, this means bringing together the important concepts that we can, so to speak, plug policy into. So I have sought to write about the key concepts, relationships and mechanisms that underpin and act as the grounding for housing finance.

Having done with the first edition – and it was very much a case of good riddance: textbooks are very difficult beasts to tame – I set about looking for a new way to teach housing finance; to conceive of the subject differently in a more thematic and conceptual manner. I had become frustrated with the dry tenure-by-tenure approach, with its description of particular parochial mechanisms, and so had my students. Watching students yawn has a toxic effect after a while. So what I wanted to do was spice it up a bit – but still no glove puppet – and avoid the disconnected tenure-based approach, which tended to become overly descriptive and to decontextualise the subject, making it appear separate from the mainstream of housing policy. Housing finance was something that you did towards the end of your programme of study, to be got through, to be endured, and so was not properly integrated into housing thinking.

There is indeed a school of thought that says that housing finance is to be endured rather than enjoyed. We might refer to this as the Presbyterian view of housing finance. Housing finance is seen as a dour subject in which students are forced to pour over numbers presented in columns and to manipulate them, all the while being closely observed by their teacher to make sure they don't smile or talk to each other.

But this is not what I take housing finance to be. Of course it is necessary to understand particular funding mechanisms and to appreciate the need for financial management, but these are the parochial activities of managing an organisation. It is my view that it is quite straightforward to find the important data and descriptions of particular mechanisms. This is provided on government websites, through reading the professional housing press and through attending short training courses. What is harder to gain and to appreciate is an understanding of the background, the context: the 'why' and 'why not' rather than the 'what'. Therefore this book seeks to provide the 'why' and 'why not', to show why housing finance has to be as it is, what the constraints and possibilities are, and how particular financial mechanisms do not operate in a vacuum, but in a highly complex and dynamic environment in which nothing stays the same for long and in which the understanding of households, policy makers, practitioners and politicians is inevitably limited.

Therefore what I take housing finance to be is the study of how the housing activity of individuals is supported, managed, encouraged and controlled through the use of financial resources. It is the study of how these resources can and are being used; how they can be channelled in particular ways. It is about why certain methods of funding and support work better than others, and are seen as more successful. It is concerned with the effects of funding in particular ways. Finally, it seeks to deal with the political, economic and social implications of all this. Housing finance, therefore, is the study of the relationship between housing markets and government's engagement with them. I refer to this as a *political economy approach to housing finance*, and, unlike the Presbyterian approach, this one is pure joy!

It might be stated in response to this justification that the result is that there is very little of what is traditionally taken to be housing finance in this book. On one level this is quite true and this is an inevitable corollary of the approach taken. Yet I would stress again that the emphasis in this book is on the word *understanding*. The purpose is to contextualise housing finance mechanisms and policies within a political economy approach that takes seriously the interaction between markets and government action.

There is, though, a more pragmatic reason for this approach. As the first edition of the book got older, it became more out of date: mechanisms changed, priorities moved on, and even the name of government departments changed, and I became increasingly frustrated. In particular, I had to offer a health warning to my students about the book's contents, which led some of them to ask why I still tried to persuade them to buy it. Several students were taken aback when I corrected them for being out of date, and they responded that they had found the information in my book, and so it must be right (or else I was an idiot). Now one might argue that a rapidly changing environment provides the opportunity for regular updating and all the royalties that this involves. Well, perhaps, but some of us have lives to lead and, as perverse as it may appear, writing housing finance books does not help that much in paying the mortgage.

This edition is therefore very different from the first edition. I have used some of the same material, but it is very much re-ordered and there are considerable changes to both structure and content. The thrust of the book is more conceptual and does not attempt to deal comprehensively with just one housing system. It is less detailed, but also less specific. It is focused on 'why' and not so much on 'what'. But anyone can take a mechanism and apply the template I have devised here to analyse it. Hopefully, therefore, the book will have a longer shelf-life and I won't have to provide a health warning to my students in a couple of years' time.

However, most of the examples on financial mechanisms and policies in chapters 5 and 6 are still from the UK. I can justify this by saying that I am an Englishman, and an Anglophile at that, so I felt that to write authoritatively I needed to stick with what I know best. Also I wanted the book to have a narrative flow to it that shows housing finance in all its complexity, and this is helped by sticking largely to one example. Having said that, much of the material, particularly in the first four chapters, has been written to have a general applicability.

One of the biggest problems with a textbook is objectivity: to be balanced and give a comprehensive and rounded view of the subject. Like everyone who writes on housing I have certain positions, hobby-horses, conceits and prejudices; things I see as important, even if this is seen as quirky by others. Of course the glib answer to any complaints about bias or not taking an issue seriously enough is to tell the accuser to write their own book, but I don't really want anyone else to do this as it is hard to sell enough copies as it is. So I must justify what I am doing and why.

The problem is essentially about how committed one is to writing a textbook and whether it ends up being unbalanced as a result. But my problem in looking at other texts, and the first edition of *Understanding Housing Finance* is as guilty as any other, is that they tend to focus far too much on state provision and not enough on the role of markets. This is partly because of the institutional nature of housing teaching, with its bias towards social housing. But it is also due to the commitment of most housing academics, who are interested in social change and improving social conditions, and therefore concentrate on the gaps and the problems and how they can be sorted out. Government action can be seen as the means of responding to problems and so that is what housing teaching focuses upon. Yet most housing, in most places, is provided through markets, and the role of government is in supporting or maintaining market activity. It is my contention, therefore, that the way in which housing finance is taught in places like the UK, and therefore how it is represented in the literature, is too much based on social provision. Probably 70 per cent of the first edition of this book was on social provision, yet it makes up less than 20 per cent of England's housing stock.

So this edition is more balanced in that it looks at housing more broadly. In particular, there is a fuller conceptual discussion, with much more on the role of markets, a thorough critique of the role of government and a general focus on the principles of housing finance, based on the roles played by markets and government.

Even though I think it is a much more balanced approach, I have no doubt that this view will be contested and critics will see this book as less balanced than the first edition. This is largely because it *does* discuss markets more fully and undertakes a fuller critique of the role of government. In other words, it will be seen as unbalanced precisely because I do not focus the vast majority of my attention on state action and minority provision.

This does not mean that there is no or only a little discussion of the role of government: I would suggest that the actions of government take up 40 to 50 per cent of the book, instead of the 70 per cent of the first edition. But I see this balance as about right, and that the need to consider the role of markets and the part played by choice in housing decision making is necessary and essential.

I have been accused, much to my own amusement, of being a 'market idealist' (Cole, 2007). Apparently, this is something very bad to be accused of and puts me in with some disreputable company. However, as I have stated, my aim in this book is to provide a balanced view, and not to push a particular agenda. Instead what I merely seek to do is to take markets seriously. I am aware that this might place me outside the consensus which sees state provision as the norm and markets as dangerous beasts to be controlled. So, whilst others may accuse me of idealism, I am quite happy to take this particular route. Indeed, my criticism of the consensus is precisely that it takes an idealistic view of social provision and ignores the reality of how housing systems actually operate, particularly the residualised provision in the UK.

This justification brings me to the narrative structure of the book. At the centre of the discussion, as I explain in chapter 1, is the relationship between markets and government. This is where I outline the political economy approach to housing finance. I start by considering need and choice (chapter 2), which are often seen as ciphers and as justifications for government intervention and market activity. I then consider markets (chapter 3) and government action (chapter 4) in some detail. But I am aware that the situation is rather more complex than just a duality between the two: it is not the case that they are polar opposites, but rather they are better seen as dependent antagonists. By that I mean, whilst they may well be opposed, or seen as such, one depends on the other, and this needs to be recognised and appreciated.

It is this situation that has motivated the structure of chapters 5 and 6 of this book. Instead of using a tenure-by-tenure approach, I have sought to look at housing finance mechanisms and tenures thematically. Indeed there are essentially two themes – one for each chapter. Chapter 5 looks at how government uses housing finance policy to influence markets. I want to portray this as the traditional form of government intervention. However, there is now another form that has become increasingly important, and this is discussed in chapter 6. This new form of intervention is where government uses market or commercial disciplines to influence, reform and control the public sector. I want to suggest that there has been a development in housing finance from influencing markets to using market disciplines to control state provision. Now, this may not really be introducing the market into government, but rather what politicians take to be 'the market'; it may be that they are just using those elements that they see as amenable to create the sort of compliance they want, and so we can question how much of the so-called 'choice agenda' and 'public sector reform' is actually genuine and about creating change. Yet, whether it is serious or not, it is an important phenomenon and needs to be explored. At least it is an important symbolic change.

This does not mean that the old form of government intervention has stopped; rather it has been overlaid with a new form. The reason for this is that government intervention is now so ingrained, and the structures apparently so natural, that it is almost impossible to envisage their absence. Government is now so involved in housing provision that it is difficult, if not impossible, to imagine its absence, and this means that market disciplines can be used as a weapon of control and to ensure that the public sector is kept in check and fulfils the government's intentions, which are often nakedly political and based on control over resources. We can characterise the position by stating that social provision is costly and unpopular, whilst owner occupation is popular but costly.

What all this means – and this I take to be a very important point – is that market disciplines are being introduced not by government withdrawing or omitting to carry out certain actions and interventions and leaving them to markets, but by government intervention itself. State provision is so pervasive that the only way of introducing market provision in housing is through government action. This, of course, is somewhat perverse, particularly if there is an antagonism between them.

But perhaps one explanation for this phenomenon is precisely the weakness, the ineffectuality of government intervention in housing. Individual choice and market provision in many developed countries is now so dominant a part of individual expectations, that the only realistic option for government is to ape the market. This is an argument that I seek to develop in the latter part of the book and, in doing so, to develop some sort of commentary on government intervention and its efficacy.

I once said at a conference as I stood to present a paper on the UK Housing Benefit system, that what I was about to talk about was Kant on housing finance. I had spent a good deal of time reading the works of the eighteenth century German philosopher, Immanuel Kant, in preparation for my book, *A Social Philosophy of Housing*, and as the paper I was about to deliver was using many of the same ideas, I thought I would set the scene. But I also thought I was being clever – after all, what has an eighteenth century German idealist philosopher got to do with Housing Benefit? But I should have known better for, quick as a flash, an eminent professor of social policy retorted, 'Do you mean Kant with a "k" or a "c"?' Unable to come up with anything suitable in response all I could say was, 'Only time will tell.' But this cliché applies now as well. The point, however, is that, whilst we might see housing as an eminently practical subject, and housing finance especially so, we should not forget that concepts and ideas matter and this is because they show that change is possible; they help us to understand that there are alternatives and that things need not be as they are. Of course, this does not make the change happen, but it does force us to stop and think, or at least it should do. Therefore a few highfaluting ideas mixed in with the policy discussion is no bad thing and I make no apology for basing much of this discussion on concepts rather than policy mechanisms.

This does not, I hope, make this edition any less readable than the first one. It was gratifying when reviewers and, more importantly, students said how readable and accessible the first edition was. I have tried to keep to that approach and retain the accessibility. I will admit that certain parts of the book may be a bit harder going than the rest, but I hope the activities will help; I can claim that I have tried most of this material, including the conceptual discussion in chapter 2, on my students and all of them survived the crossing (even if I did have to go back in to rescue the stragglers!).

A number of tables are provided in each chapter. In most cases these are used to summarise key points that are discussed in more detail in the text. The aim of these tables is to offer a quick point of reference for what I consider to be important parts of the argument.

There are a number of points for thought, reflections and questions distributed throughout the chapters, which I have referred to as 'think points'. Some of these points are capable of being answered definitively, but most are meant as points for reflection or discussion. Some might be used for class or web-based discussions or as assignment topics. But my main aim with this material has been to try to focus the surrounding discussion in the text.

Finally, I have to acknowledge the help and support of a number of people. First, I am grateful to my students for their responses, comments and challenges. Even their puzzled looks have helped to sift out what did not work and what did. In particular, I thank those students who suffered my 'Housing Markets and the State' module in 2007/08, who were guinea pigs for this approach to the material. I hope they have recovered.

Second, my colleague Tim Brown has offered many comments and asides on my ideas; I am grateful for his robust attitude to housing issues and for the constant support he gives his colleagues. He is truly a good man. It has also been a delight that Mike Oxley has returned to De Montfort for at least some of his time. I have always welcomed his views on housing finance issues and he always provides challenging and thought-provoking comments, which I initially try to argue against but find in the end that I should not. And to have the opportunity to discuss housing finance in Delft rather than Leicester has also been a pleasure.

I am particularly grateful to Katy Low and her colleagues at Routledge for their support and encouragement of this project and for making it go so smoothly. I would also like to thank the four anonymous reviewers who, much to my surprise, all supported my ideas for this new edition. Is it a record to get four academics to all agree on the same thing?

Finally, to family. My sister-in-law, Sheila, has proofread the text and made countless improvements and saved much embarrassment. Not for the first time, and probably not for the last, my wife, B, and daughters, Helen and Rachel, have put up with my obsessive and unsociable way of working. They have been forced to listen to my anxieties and progress reports on this book. So I thank them for listening – or at least pretending to – and for nodding occasionally and smiling as I drone on. And a very last point: in April 2008, B and Sheila lost their dad, and my daughters their granddad. Therefore it seems only right to dedicate this book to Tom, who really was a lovely man.

Peter King
June 2008

1

Understanding housing finance

Learning outcomes

- Why we need to know about housing finance.
- What housing finance is.
- The centrality of the issues of quality and access.
- The political economy approach to housing finance.

A nightmare

Imagine you wake up and find yourself not in your bed or even in your own home, but in the middle of a jungle. You are in an unfamiliar and hostile environment. There are no roads, no buildings, no signs whatsoever of human civilisation. And it gets worse. You have no means to communicate: no mobile phone or laptop; you have no food or drink and just the clothes on your back. You really are in trouble! You are back in the Stone Age.

How would you live?

Of course, you might not survive long: if the cold or hunger doesn't get you, a wild animal might. But let's assume you've watched the right TV programmes and you know what to do, and so you survive.

What would you do?

You would look for shelter, perhaps in a cave, or make a rudimentary shack with branches. You might learn to make a fire to keep you warm, to light up your shelter, and to cook the food you might have caught or gathered. And over time as your skills develop, you learn more and more and get better at surviving. You make your shelter watertight, stronger and safer.

But how much further could you take your life? How much could you improve your situation?

You might be lucky and meet others in a similar situation who aren't hostile, or you might be spotted and rescued. But what if you remain there, on your own and having to depend on your wits?

What sort of life would it be?

But now you wake up properly and feel with relief that the nightmare is over. You find you are still in bed, with the clock ticking nearby, perhaps the sound of gentle breathing next to you and the normal sounds of a house resting at night. You feel a sense of relief that you have plenty of food and drink in the fridge, light and heat at the flick of a switch, money in the bank and credit cards in your pocket, and the ready ability to communicate with people, either face-to-face or via the various bits of technology you have lying around and take for granted.

And this is entirely the point of this little thought experiment. That we take what is around us for granted; we just assume the technology and amenities are there and will always be there. But these things are not *just there*. Someone or something has to provide them and we, at some time in our lives, have also had to make the effort to get them. So now that we are back in our safe little world, perhaps we ought to think of what it is we need to maintain our own lifestyles.

Obviously we need the money to buy and maintain our dwelling and all the other things we need for our lives. But it is not just the money. There have to be the physical resources and materials available to build our houses, to use as food and so on. We also need lots of energy to heat our dwellings, to get us from place to place and run the industries and services we rely upon. But we – or rather the society we live in – need the knowledge that allows us to make things properly and to try to control our environment. Finally, we need some leisure to be able to sit back and enjoy our time and use the things around us. We have to be in a situation whereby we are not continually struggling for survival but can take our standard of living for granted and just enjoy it.

This suggests that the life we lead is complex and involves many different facets that need to come together just to allow us to get out of the shower and walk down the stairs to put the kettle on. The life we are used to is possible because of co-operation on a large scale. We rely on others to provide the goods and services we need. We want hot water on tap, light at the flick of a switch, petrol in the pump and food on the supermarket shelves, but we may not be aware of how any of this comes about, and what's more, we really don't need to know.

But this means that we have to rely on the co-operation of strangers. The lifestyles that we have necessitate a reliance on people we have not met, and will never meet, who live in different parts of the world and are going about their lives in sweet ignorance of our existence. This is what economists call a *disembedded economy* (Levine, 1995); in which our consumption of goods and services is separate from their production and in which we do not provide everything for ourselves.

But if people don't know we exist, how can they possibly know what we need and want? How can we co-operate with those of whom we are ignorant? The answer is that we need some form of co-ordination that allows the needs of strangers to be met. This co-ordination might take the form of a market, where people come together to buy and sell, or it might be undertaken by government that plans for the needs of its citizens.

This discussion, starting with a very simple thought experiment, has introduced some of the key concepts and issues that will be discussed in this book. In particular, we have started to consider what it is that we need in order to lead the sorts of lives we are used to and how this might come about. We have to co-operate with others in order for the full complexity of our lives to be fulfilled, and this needs a high degree of co-ordination. But how is this achieved, and how can we understand it? It is the aim of this book to try to answer this question.

The aim of this book is to concentrate on the *normative* basis of housing systems: about what we can and should do for ourselves and what we need others for; about how we can and should live and what this entails in terms of the provision and co-ordination of resources. This will involve some detailed consideration of particular housing finance mechanisms, but the emphasis will be more on the reasons for particular forms of provision and how these link with the needs and choices of individual households.

I have chosen to call such an approach the *political economy of housing finance*. In the rest of this chapter I shall explore what this means and why it offers an important way into appreciating the complexities of housing systems and the interdependencies that households have. The first task, however, is to define just what housing finance is. Having done this, we can then start to appreciate how it ought to be studied.

What do we mean by 'housing finance'?

Put simply, housing finance is what allows for the production and consumption of housing. It refers to the money we use to build and maintain the nation's housing stock. But it also refers to the money we need to pay for it, in the form of rents, mortgage loans and repayments.

There is a tendency to think that housing finance is all about government subsidies, such as capital grants, housing allowances and tax relief. These are all important, or have been, and we shall indeed spend parts of this book considering the various forms of government subsidy. However, we need to be aware that there is more to housing finance than subsidies.

The majority of households in the UK, USA and parts of Europe are owner occupiers who pay for their housing from their own income. Therefore much housing finance is found privately, mainly from earned income. Of course, a household's income is normally used to repay a loan provided by a commercial bank or building society. This is another important source of housing finance. In addition, households use their own money and borrow in order to fund repairs and improvements to their dwellings. They also spend money on decoration, furnishings and fittings.

But private finance has also become increasingly important in the social rented sector. In the UK, for instance, housing associations have used private finance alongside government subsidy to develop new social rented housing. Social landlords therefore have to borrow from banks and building societies, just like private households.

So we need to be aware that housing finance consists of more than subsidies from government. It involves the far larger sums spent by households and housing organisations that are derived from income and from borrowing. But there are two further facets of housing finance we need to consider.

First, housing is a store of wealth, and thus we need to be aware of the fact that the housing stock is an asset that can be used by its owners. Individuals can, and do, tap into this wealth in order, say, to set up a small business, pay school and university fees for their children or enjoy their retirement. Landlords can use their assets as security for future development. Thus housing wealth can allow households and landlords to develop housing and non-housing activities.

The second issue returns us to the role of government. Because housing is so expensive and so valuable an asset – as well as being so important to our well-being – government feels the need to regulate housing finance. It can do this through interest rates that affect mortgage repayments, and by controlling rents through rent controls and regulating standards, which impose costs on landlords. Therefore we need to consider not just the money that government spends on housing, but the costs that its actions impose on the various players involved in the production and consumption of housing.

A consideration of what housing finance is also tells us where the money comes from. It shows us that, whilst some finance comes from government, we need also to consider other sources, such as earned income and private finance. Table 1.1 summarises what I take housing finance to include.

Table 1.1   What housing finance is and where it comes from

- Government subsidies to landlords and households.

- Households' own income used to provide, maintain and improve their housing and the amenities within it.

- Private finance from mortgage lenders and financial institutions to fund house purchases and social housing development.

- The wealth stored in housing, which is used to fund housing and non-housing activities.

- Government regulation of housing, which imposes or limits costs, such as building regulations and rent controls.

Why do we need housing finance?

Table 1.1 also begins to tell us why we might need housing finance. I would suggest that we need it for at least four reasons, highlighted in Table 1.2. Without finance we could not achieve any of these objectives.

But this offers only a partial answer to the question of why we need finance, in that it does not explain why government has a role. We need to appreciate this because government does not intervene in the same manner with all households. The list of facets that housing finance covers shown in Table 1.1 does not apply equally to all households. In particular, government's role differs according to households' income and therefore their ability to provide housing for themselves. In some cases government offers financial support and regulation, whilst in others (and this is the majority) it merely regulates standards. Moreover, this regulation might directly or indirectly impose costs on households, rather than providing them with financial support.

All this suggests that housing finance fulfils a more specific purpose over and above the general objectives described below. I would suggest that this purpose is to ensure a housing system that offers quality and access to all households.

Table 1.2   What housing finance is used for

- To build new dwellings.

- To cover a household's housing costs in the form of rent or mortgage repayments.

- To fund necessary maintenance and improvements to dwellings.

- To manage the housing stock to ensure it meets certain political and social objectives, such as fulfilling urgent housing need.

Quality and access

Housing is one of the most important items that we human beings need. There are many things that we would find difficult, if not impossible, to do without good quality housing. We might find it hard to find and keep a job, to learn, to maintain our health, to vote, to claim benefits we are entitled to and to initiate and maintain stable relationships.

But just because something is important, this does not mean it is always available. Like most commodities, housing comes with a price tag attached. If we want decent housing, we have to pay for it. It also follows, broadly speaking, that the better the standard of housing we want, the more it will cost us. Therefore, as standards rise, so does the cost.

One of the most important issues, then, is how we can afford the sort of housing that we want. We could say that this is simply a case of matching up our income with our aspirations and expectations and buying the best dwelling we can afford. This may be fine for those on reasonable incomes, but not for those on low incomes. Many households will lack a sufficient income to provide them with a dwelling that meets their expectations. It may well be that they could find housing of some sort, but this might not be of a standard that they, or the society of which they are a part, find acceptable.

This implies that two issues are of supreme importance. The first is *quality*. We are not content with just any type of housing; we want good quality housing that allows us to live a civilised and healthy existence. We therefore require housing to a modern standard of amenity. This standard, of course, is a relative one, in that it depends on general expectations that exist here and now. It is no good saying that households elsewhere in the world manage with less or that our grandparents were brought up without central heating and modern appliances.

The second issue follows on from this, and is about *access*. We might readily agree on what constitutes a good quality dwelling for us here and now. We can describe the particular amenities and standards that the modern dwelling should have. But that doesn't mean that everybody has such a dwelling. Many households might not be able to afford one.

There is a clear trade-off between quality and access, in that, generally speaking, the higher the quality, the fewer will be able to gain access to it. Quality comes at a cost, and this limits access. There is, then, a gap that needs to be filled between the aspirations people have for good quality housing and their ability to access it because of a lack of income. This is where housing finance comes in, by acting as the bridge over this gap.

Therefore the true purpose of housing finance – and the historical reason why the state has intervened to provide subsidies – is to ensure that all citizens gain access to good quality housing.

A political approach to housing finance

But a definition like this can only take us so far. When discussing the issue of quality, it became clear that we could not define it absolutely but only *relatively*. What we consider to be good quality housing depends upon on our expectations and the norms of the society we are part of. These change over time as we become more (or less) affluent, and as our society becomes more (or less) open to external influences. However, it is not helpful to talk of the housing conditions of 50 years ago, or in other countries, as if they can be the models for how we do, or wish to, live now. What matters is the housing we can reasonably expect and aspire to here and now and whether we are able to attain it.

This means that we should pay attention to the objective physical conditions of housing in our society and the particular mechanisms that provide and sustain that housing. But it also means we should be aware of what it is that households feel that they want and need. Our concern should not merely be to describe what is currently happening with regard to housing finance, but also to understand why things are as they are, and what pressures exist that both create particular mechanisms and force them to change.

I would argue that these pressures come from two sources, which sometimes interact and at other times might be conflictual. On the one hand, we have the actions of government, which initiates, controls and regulates mechanisms; on the other hand, there are the actions of individual households in markets who use particular mechanisms, are incentivised or limited by them and whose combined behaviour can influence the operation of mechanisms, as well, of course, as the continued existence of any particular government.

Housing policy is thus part of a wider set of relationships between government and individuals. This is the domain of *political economy*. According to Adam Smith, who is commonly seen as the founder of the discipline, political economy has two distinct objectives:

> First, to provide a plentiful revenue or subsistence for the people, or more properly to enable them to provide such a revenue or subsistence for themselves; and secondly, to supply the state or commonwealth with a revenue sufficient for the public services.
>
> (Smith, 1981, p. 428)

Smith assumes two important things. The first is that individuals should be able to provide for themselves. Households should be able to find the wherewithal to meet their wants and needs. But, second, Smith assumes that there is a need for government action to provide public services. This immediately shows the relationship between the individual and the state. Smith sees the state as facilitating individual action, whilst, of course, the revenue of the state can only be derived from the actions of individuals themselves. It is only through individual households thriving that the state can raise any finance through taxation in order to fund necessary public services.

Political economy makes a particular assumption about the nature of a society, and this is one we have already mentioned: that societies are complex and depend on co-operation between strangers. Accordingly, Levine (1995) has stated that political economy is the study of *disembedded economies*. It is precisely the analysis of those economies that are separated from the household and are thus subject to conjecture, thought and action. The key relationships are therefore not within households but through markets, where strangers come together to meet their wants and needs.

Indeed a contemporary approach to political economy is principally concerned with markets and government action, and particularly with how one influences the other. Levine suggests that one way of seeing the roles of markets and government is through the distinction between *wants* and *needs*. Wants are things 'we choose for ourselves as a way of expressing who we are' (pp. 31–2). Wants are often specific and particular; they are best met through individual decision making and through a market system. It is where we wish to make choices rather than having a standardised solution imposed upon us. As many of the things we want (as opposed to need) are not imperatives – our life does not depend on them – there is no need for standardisation or imposition. The aim of expressing our wants is quite often a means of stating our differences from others. This emphasis on wants, however, is most commonly expressed through the idea of choice. This is important, as choice carries within it the idea of a purposive action: to choose implies that we are doing something rather than passively accepting a situation dictated from outside.

Needs, however, are things 'imposed upon me independently of my will' (p. 31). Wants are connected to markets as the vehicle for choice and self-expression. Needs can be met by uniformity but wants cannot. Needs also often have a greater imperative attached to them in that they are immediate and have serious consequences if neglected, such as serious illness or starvation. Thus it is often argued that certain goods and services should be provided at the point of immediate need, regardless of an individual's ability to pay. But if we lack the ability to pay, this presumes that there is some other body that can ensure that our need is met, and this body is usually government.

Therefore to concentrate on needs leads us to contemplate government action, whilst a concern for wants is more likely to leave us satisfied with markets. This is, of course, a simplistic distinction, as we shall see when we discuss need and choice in more detail in the next chapter. However, this dichotomy is an important one for political economy as it helps us understand the respective roles of government and individual households. In political terms, that distinction matters because stating whether one has a need or a choice has implications for who is responsible for dealing with the situation. If we are in need of a serious operation, then we are unlikely to be able to treat ourselves, and so the responsibility falls on some other agency. However, if we have neglected to pay our rent and chosen to spend the money on alcohol, can we reasonably expect someone else to help us? This is the sort of question that a political economy approach to housing finance can help us deal with.

In general terms, the political economy approach taken in this book rests on three core propositions. First, housing finance mechanisms operate within dynamic, open systems. This means that factors external to housing systems (inflation, unemployment, poverty, etc.) impact on housing, and thus problems cannot be solved by purely internal processes. Housing problems can often be solved only by using non-housing solutions. Second, the impact and effect of unintended consequences on policy outcomes are considerable. Because of the complexity of housing systems, not all eventualities can be predicted or taken into account. This places a severe limitation on the policy process itself. The most destabilising issues in politics are those that have not been foreseen. Housing is not immune from these events, and we need to be aware that they will happen, even though we can never predict what they will be and when they will occur. Many of the most important housing phenomena, such as the decline of private renting, were not foreseen.

Third, individual households have a considerable impact on housing outcomes, and thus we need to go beyond the study of institutions and structural forces. We have to be aware of the impact of issues such as need and choice and how the behaviour of households and landlords meshes into policy.

These propositions are central to the discussion in this book and place particular stress on the idea of *complexity*. We can show just how complex housing systems are by attempting to model them.

A simple model of complex systems

I believe we can model housing systems to show three distinct levels that have different, if overlapping, functions. These three levels are identified in Table 1.3.

Of course, Table 1.3 is indeed a considerable simplification of actual housing processes. The three levels are not independent of each other, but

Table 1.3   Three levels of housing politics

Level	Agent
Planning	Central government
Implementation	Social and private landlords, mortgage lenders, professionals
Personal	Households

are related. Moreover, these relationships are unpredictable, not only because each level affects the others, but because many external factors also influence the outcomes at each level.

Yet, by holding on to this model, we can understand the political relationships that operate within housing and gain a fuller appreciation of how systems work. It recognises some extremely important facets of the housing system that we need to appreciate. First, planning and implementation take place at different levels and are undertaken by different organisations. Governments make policy, but it is implemented by other organisations at another level. Hence there is the possibility of political conflict, divergence of interest, and misunderstanding and misinterpretation. It is important to realise that there is not necessarily a shared interest across all three levels.

Second, housing is experienced at the personal level, and the process therefore does not stop at the implementation level. We need to understand the impact at the personal level, and it is primarily (though not exclusively) at this level that we can measure success or failure. Third, because there are three distinct levels, there can be a multiplicity of external factors that impact on the housing process. Moreover, because the three levels are functionally interrelated, an external influence at one level can influence behaviour at the other levels. An example of this is the impact of increasing unemployment at the personal level and the consequences this might have for the policy and implementation levels as households struggle with their housing costs and seek cheaper alternatives.

Next, this implies that concentrating only on one level will give us a misleading view on how the housing process operates. We would never be able to explain housing phenomena satisfactorily by concentrating on just one level. But, finally, because we cannot predict the influences or pre-empt the effect of the various interrelationships, we can never fully appreciate the housing system in all its complexity, except, of course, by hindsight.

The model shown in Table 1.3 is indeed, therefore, a simplification of what is an extremely complex set of relationships, and one that may well be immune to a complete understanding. One of the key arguments of this book stresses the complexity of housing finance systems and the consequent limitations this places on policy making. However, this does not mean that we should not try to understand more than we currently do about housing, and it is only by appreciating and accepting our limitations that we can make any progress at all.

Understanding housing finance

This book, then, offers a political economy approach to housing finance. What this means is that we cannot even attempt to understand housing finance without three things. These are stated in Table 1.4.

We cannot understand housing finance as an isolated set of issues. Indeed, I would suggest that it is quite straightforward to obtain up-to-date data on housing and to learn about the key mechanisms. What is more important, however, is to appreciate the reasons for particular structures and how these relate to the normative behaviour of individuals within complex systems in which any one person's understanding is limited and no one person or agency is able to exert a decisive level of control.

We do not live a subsistence life, and in most cases would not wish to. We would find the type of life discussed at the start of this chapter unpleasant and even frightening. But it would be a very simple life and one, moreover, in which we would be forced to concentrate on our needs rather than looking to exercise choice. But we do not just want a basic shelter. We feel the need for a modern, civilised life with high quality housing that allows us to fulfil our aspirations. As citizens in a modern society we want to be able to choose where we live, who with, and in what sort of dwelling. We want

Table 1.4 Understanding housing finance

- We need an appreciation of the key concepts of need, choice and responsibility that underpin both public policy and private action.

- We need to understand how all the parts of the housing system fit together and to appreciate that the growth in certain tenures has been at the expense of others and that some households are helped from the income of others.

- We should understand that politics involves exercising expectations and aspirations, as well as economic resources. Tenants and owner occupiers are also voters, parents, homebuilders and citizens. Importantly, they carry out these roles concurrently and without seeking prior permission from government, landlord or mortgage lender. They are likely to see these roles as more important than whom they are a tenant of or whom they make their mortgage payments to. Regardless of tenure and ownership, a dwelling is always somebody's home.

to be comfortable and secure. But this imposes costs, and these fall not just on us but on the broader society. That is why we have formal structures of housing provision and why we need finance, and the more complex our lives become the more complex are the arrangements needed to support them. And this, in turn, means we have to work harder to understand how housing finance systems work.

Further reading

A useful general text on housing finance, which concentrates on the UK, is Garnett and Perry (2005). This book has a good contextual section at the beginning and generally mixes economic analysis and accounting principles to good effect. It is a very detailed book and puts housing organisations into their broader financial contexts. It therefore takes a fundamentally different approach to the one found in this book.

For a discussion on political economy a good place to start is Levine (1995). As I state above, the founding text is Adam Smith's *The Wealth of Nations* (1981), which is very long, detailed but fascinating (take both volumes on holiday with you!).

In terms of a political economy approach to housing finance, my book *Housing, Individuals and the State* (King, 1998) explicitly takes this approach, without being as comprehensive as this book in its coverage of housing finance issues. See also King and Oxley's *Housing: Who Decides?* (2000) for a debate between the political and the economic approaches to housing. There was a time when 'political economy' meant 'Marxist', and an example of this from the housing literature is Ball (1983).

2

Need, choice and responsibility

Learning outcomes

- A conceptual approach to housing finance.
- The importance of need as a justification for housing provision.
- Why choice is increasingly important.
- How we can apply responsibility to housing.

Introduction

Housing finance, as we have seen, is about ensuring access to good quality housing. But providing a quality product is expensive and this makes access harder, particularly for those on low incomes. What this suggests is that we need to be concerned with *how* households are able to gain access to high-quality housing. Gaining access is, of course, a question of resources, of having the money and materials available. But it is also a question of *who* controls the resources and *where* the money comes from; or, in other words, whose money is being used to provide good quality housing for all households? Do we expect households to sort out their housing for themselves, or is it a problem that is beyond them and so needs the intervention of government? Can we leave the provision of good quality housing to markets and households using their own income, or does government need to assist this process?

We tend to talk quite glibly about government spending and about the demands of the taxpayer. We suggest that we have to weigh up the interests of the taxpayer against those of patients, rail travellers, applicants for social housing and others who seek to benefit from government funding. Yet we need to remember that all government expenditure comes from households and businesses. Government's money derives from income tax paid by individuals; from duties on goods like tobacco, alcohol and petrol; from taxes on consumption, such as VAT; and from corporation tax levied on the profits of businesses. So, properly speaking, the taxpayer is also the patient wanting access to a new drug treatment, the commuter wanting a seat on the train home from work, the parent of school-age children and the member of a household wanting a new dwelling. Government, to coin a phrase, has no money of its own – *it is all ours.*

This means we are paying for services, such as health, education, roads and housing that we might directly benefit from. However, this raises the question of whether we could provide these things for ourselves, and if we feel we can, why is government doing it for us? If we are capable of earning and spending the money, why does government take it from us and then spend it on things for us?

An obvious answer to this question is that our taxes are also being used for the benefit of others who are not themselves earning. Indeed, it may be that we, because we are very young or very old, ill or vulnerable in some way so that we cannot earn, are benefiting from the taxes paid by others. This is particularly the case with social housing, which has traditionally been allocated on the basis of need and so will tend to have a higher proportion of low income households.

But this is not the sole reason for government taxing and spending. It may be that the things we need, like health care or education for our children, are very expensive and we would struggle to afford them. Hence we might see government action as a form of insurance, whereby money is taken from us on a regular basis to make sure that provision is there for us when we need it and regardless of whether we can pay for it there and then.

Another answer is that there may be some forms of provision that are very necessary, like national defence and security, roads and railways, but that we are just not capable of providing for ourselves. So, left to ourselves, these items would not be provided either at all or in sufficient quantities.

Finally, there may be some types of help that we would not be prepared to provide directly ourselves. We might admit that paedophiles or serial killers have to be housed somewhere, but many of us would not be prepared to volunteer our own money for the purpose. But this form of provision can be 'hidden' within the much greater total of government expenditure, and, as it probably accounts for much less than 1 per cent of the amount we pay in tax, we don't notice.

These questions over the use of taxation and the role of government lead us away from the everyday concerns of bricks and mortar and towards more conceptual considerations. However, they are no less important for being conceptual, in that they concern the ability that we have to provide for ourselves and the role that government has in protecting and providing for us.

There are three concepts in particular that I wish to explore here: *need*, *choice* and *responsibility*. I see these concepts as being crucial for any understanding of the relationship between households and government and therefore the role of housing finance. In this chapter I want to focus on these concepts and try to address three rather large questions:

- What do we mean when we say we need something? How do we know that we need it? Are we the best ones to judge?
- Can we all choose where and in what we live? Should we always have a choice? What about children and adults with learning difficulties?
- What happens if we choose badly or are found to be incapable? Who should be held responsible if we fail, especially if our failure leaves our dependents and ourselves destitute?

These concepts of need, choice and responsibility are fundamental to housing finance, and I would even go so far as to say that they should be seen as more important than specific mechanisms or funding arrangements. This is because they form the underpinnings to financial systems. Social housing has traditionally been justified on the basis of need, and dwellings have been allocated according to needs-based criteria. Likewise, governments tend to plan for future provision on the basis of the need for dwellings due to factors such as migration and new household formation. The most basic justification for state intervention in housing and planning is that there are urgent needs that are being left unmet by markets.

But, if we look at housing policies across the developed world over the last twenty years, we see that choice has become increasingly important as an organising principle. We can see this in the promotion of owner occupation, but also in the reduction in subsidies to landlords and their replacement by housing allowances paid to households. Housing subsidies are now being used to allow households to make choices over their housing. Households are being cast in the role of customers and consumers rather than passive or vulnerable recipients of state welfare.

But this raises the question of how far households should be able to exercise choice and how far this is compatible with the comprehensive welfare systems in many developed countries. Is it possible to allow choices but also ensure that needs are being met? What if households choose badly: does this mean that the state is no longer responsible for ensuring their needs are fulfilled? If individuals make the wrong choices, can we simply say they are to blame and therefore they should be responsible for sorting out the matter for themselves?

But we can use the notion of responsibility in two very distinct ways. We can see the term as bearing on the actions of individuals such that these individuals have a *personal* responsibility for what they have done or failed to do. But we also talk of a *social* responsibility, meaning that we have a duty to meet the needs of others, either directly or through state agencies to which we contribute through our taxes. Responsibility can therefore be about being held to account for one's actions, but also about showing a direct concern for the needs of others.

These three concepts of need, choice and responsibility are about who makes decisions about housing and the consequences that flow from those decisions. They are integral to any discussion of the role of markets and the state, in that choice and personal responsibility can bolster the role of the market, whilst need and social responsibility can be used to justify government intervention in housing. Indeed, as we saw in chapter 1, Levine (1995) distinguishes between the market and government on the basis of the distinction between needs and wants, between imperatives and choices, and this implies that responsibility should be apportioned in different ways.

A further reason for looking at these three concepts is that they are frequently used by politicians and policy makers to justify their actions. In the UK, proposals to reform Housing Benefit were promoted under a banner of 'choice and responsibility' (DWP, 2002) and choice-based lettings have been introduced as the standard means of letting social housing (Brown and King, 2005), a policy that has already been introduced across most municipalities in the Netherlands (Oxley *et al.*, 2008). Likewise, countries such as Australia, New Zealand and the USA have shifted to housing finance systems based squarely on personal subsidies involving a degree of conditionality, which seeks to inculcate personal responsibility rather than a reliance on state welfare (Hirst, 2007; Kemp, 2007a).

So, whilst this chapter is rather conceptual, the discussion does link directly with policy. However, all too frequently these concepts are used as if they pose no problems. It is assumed that government policy can create choice or that individuals can become more responsible because government says so (King, 2006). What tends to be missing from policy debates involving choice, need and responsibility is any attempt to define these concepts. But it is only by defining concepts that we can start to understand them fully and so appreciate the possibilities and limits of their application to housing. This chapter therefore seeks to provide some definitions of these concepts and draw out possibilities and limits. This, I believe, will allow us a fuller understanding of housing finance.

Think point What do you really need?

Make a list of the things that you are certain you need – those things you believe you could not live without.

Having done this, choose one item from the list and ask yourself what it would mean to give it up. Do you really need it? Can you really not live without it? Go through your entire list and see how many you are left with. What sort of life would you have?

Need

As I have stated, the notion of need is central to most definitions of social housing. For example, one of Harloe's three points in defining social housing states:

> It is administratively allocated according to some conception of 'need' (although often not to those objectively in the worst housing conditions). Ability to pay can be important but, in contrast to private market provision, is usually not the dominant determinant of allocation.
>
> (Harloe, 1995, p. 13)

The idea of need is used to distinguish social housing from private market provision. Likewise, Cole and Furbey (1994) make a similar point when they quote the Inquiry into British Housing (1990), which argued that the term 'social rented housing' implies that:

> The purposes underlying provision are social rather than commercial, and that allocation will take place according to need rather than profit, and that the interest of tenants will be uppermost amongst a landlord's considerations.
>
> (Inquiry into British Housing (1990), quoted in Cole and Furbey (1994), p. 120)

The implication is that, when need is involved, it is not proper for a landlord to make a profit or to put their private gain above or even alongside the interests of tenants. Need, it is suggested, overrides commercial considerations. For this to happen, of course, housing provision would have to be organised outside markets and according to a set of principles which emphasise the tenants' interests.

But how is it possible to do this? Clearly it can only be done if it is possible to define housing need and to identify those who are to be helped. A particularly useful definition of need is that provided by Robinson:

> The quantity of housing that is required to provide accommodation of an agreed minimum standard and above for a population given its size, household composition, age distribution, etc. *without* taking into account the individual household's ability to pay for the housing assigned to it.
>
> (Robinson, 1979, pp. 55–6)

This type of definition is sometimes referred to as *geographical need*, in that it seeks to identify the housing requirements for a particular population, say within a local authority or municipality. But, of course, this definition could also be used to apply to a region or even a national population.

There are a number of important elements to this type of need. First, Robinson points to the fact that housing need requires the establishment of a particular standard of provision. This relates to the discussion we had on quality in chapter 1, where we stated that housing should be provided at a civilised standard. This may be defined in statute in terms of fitness and habitability or it might be stated in policy terms, such as the Decent Homes Standard (see Table 2.1) in England, which identifies a minimum standard for social housing. The standard, however, will change over time; for instance, the Decent Homes Standard insists on central heating and double glazing, which would not have been considered as standard in social housing in the 1960s.

Second, this definition of housing need excludes the ability to pay as a criterion. Housing need should be determined by objective conditions, such as household composition and the standard of the housing stock, and not according to income. The idea behind this is that all households should be

Table 2.1   The English Decent Homes Standard

A dwelling is decent if it:

- meets the current statutory minimum standard for housing;
- is in a reasonable state of repair;
- has reasonably modern facilities and services (age of bathroom, kitchen, etc.);
- provides a reasonable degree of thermal comfort (efficient heating and effective insulation).

---

able to gain access to housing of a certain standard and this applies regardless of income.

Third, and perhaps most significant for our discussion here, need is defined *externally*. It must to be assessed by experts from outside the particular population on the basis of formally established criteria. It is not the individual households within the population who determine their needs, but rather they are deemed to be in need by virtue of how they measure up against the particular standard that has been agreed for that population of which they are a part. It is not for individual households to determine whether they are in need, but for experts to make that judgement.

Indeed this definition is a rather impersonal one, in that it tends to look at a whole population rather than its component parts. This is a valid exercise, in that it may show the scale of a problem and allow a local housing organisation to make an informed bid for government funding. However, it does not cover the issue of need completely. We can see this when we consider the manner in which social housing is allocated. In order to do so, a population has to be disaggregated to allow for the allocation to be made. The landlord needs to be able to differentiate between rival applicants to determine who should be allocated a vacant dwelling. This, of course, could be done on the basis of 'first come, first served' or according to who agrees to pay the highest amount of rent. But if one is seeking to allocate to the most deserving or most vulnerable, the landlord has to be capable of differentiating between the needs of different households. Likewise, in means tested benefits systems there has to be some way of targeting the benefits on those who need them most.

What is needed therefore is a means of differentiating between the needs of individuals. The type of need defined by Robinson will merely identify the number and type of properties needed in an area. However, what is required is some means of deciding which households within that area should be allocated these dwellings.

Bradshaw (1972) has distinguished between four types of need that can be used to separate households. However, before discussing them, it is interesting to note that Bradshaw refers to these needs not as 'individual' but as 'social'. Social need is what society as a whole identifies as a problem or lack, which it seeks to remedy through the provision of a social service, such as social housing. So the need is social in the sense of identifying a problem that society wishes to see eradicated. However, the identification of these social needs can be used to differentiate *between* different households and so use need as a means of allocating social housing to individuals.

The first category Bradshaw identifies is *normative need*. This most closely relates to geographical need, and can be seen as what some expert or authority defines as need in a given situation; indeed it can be used to identify the needs of a population, as well as to distinguish between those within one. In essence it suggests that we identify some acceptable norm or standard to which everyone should have access; hence the similarity to Robinson's definition of defining housing need according to a *minimum standard*. It is a normative standard in that the actual level of provision is dependent on the specific time and place rather than being an absolute.

Second, Bradshaw identifies *felt need*, which refers to an individual's own assessment of their requirements. This might be assessed by surveys, question-naires or interviews, and can therefore be highly subjective. In particular, it can often be difficult to separate out a want from a need. However, such a notion of need is important in that it can provide data on consumer satisfaction and on the perceptions that consumers have of a product or an agency.

Third, we can identify *expressed need*, which is where the felt need is acted upon. This is shown by our purchasing behaviour, or by what economists call *effective demand*. But this too does not distinguish between a real need and a want: just because we have money to spend on something it does not mean we need it. However, it can be seen as a means of determining what policies and practices a social landlord undertakes and what sort of dwellings it builds. We can perhaps see choice-based lettings systems as an example of this type of need, in that applicants actually have to bid for specific properties in particular locations. This can be seen as a more accurate guide to what people need (or want) than answers to hypothetical questions in a survey.

Finally Bradshaw defines *comparative need*. This is when a comparison is made with those who are already in receipt of a service. It is when we compare those who are well housed with those in similar circumstances who are not well housed. The latter are then said to be in comparative need. This type of need emphasises equal treatment and fairness.

But what is need?

These are indeed useful categories, but what we still have not come to is a precise definition of need. All the discussion above has presupposed that we know what a need is. Yet, as the discussion on Bradshaw's four types of need shows, it can be difficult to separate a need from a want. But, if we are to take the concept of need seriously, we should have a means of separating needs from wants, otherwise we cannot justify prioritising either a particular individual or group, or the necessity for certain types of dwelling rather than others. We can see this problem by looking at the Sustainable Communities Plan (ODPM, 2003), which forms the basis for new housing provision in England. This plan identified four growth areas, all in the south of England,

and did so on the basis of the demand for housing in these areas. We might suggest that this is a form of expressed need, in which often affluent middle class households were actively showing their preferences by trying to purchase properties in certain areas. However, is it really the case that a household 'needs' a four bedroom detached house in Surrey or Cambridgeshire? We all might aspire to such a dwelling, and some people might be able to afford it, but is this really the same as a need?

On a slightly different tack, if our parents and grandparents (not to mention most of the world's population) managed without double glazing and central heating, why can't we? Why do we insist on stating that a house without certain amenities is not 'decent'? Of course, as I have suggested, we need to be aware that all definitions with regard to housing are relative, in that what matters is what we expect and aspire to in the here and now. Yet this does not mean that we are correct to call the expectation of attaining a particular standard of housing a need.

So we should seek out a precise definition of a need that helps us to distinguish between imperatives and aspirations. As we saw in chapter 1, Levine (1995) conveniently distinguishes between needs and wants. He suggests that needs are things 'imposed upon me independently of my will' (p. 31), whilst wants are things 'we choose for ourselves as a way of expressing who we are' (pp. 31–2). Wants may not be things we absolutely have to have, but they relate to our perception of ourselves, our aspirations and the status we seek to fulfil these. It is not therefore a matter of whether we have a house or not, but rather what type of house, where it is, what the neighbours think and what the house says about us. What is immediately clear is that Robinson's definition of housing need could equally refer to wants. What would determine the matter would be the actual minimum standard that is set. Modern standards, as demonstrated by the Decent Homes Standard, do not just relate to keeping us warm, dry and safe from intrusion, but go much further to include a high degree of comfort and leisure.

Levine argues that wants can and should be met through a market, whereas needs may be better met by government action. Thus wants are related to choice, but needs are not. The question, of course, is where one draws the line between a want and a need. Percy-Smith (1996) has argued that anti-collectivists and libertarians state that there is no such entity as need. What are referred to as needs are in fact individual desires and preferences. In other words, they are subjective wants that allow for no universal statements to be constructed about the general human condition. According to this view, anti-collectivists do not accept any objective notion of need as the basis for decisions about what society requires. Instead they would seek a much greater reliance on markets. Percy-Smith and her colleagues

(Percy-Smith, 1996) counter this by suggesting that need can form an empirical and objective basis for social policy, whilst admitting that there is a normative element to the formation of any concept of need.

Likewise, Doyal and Gough (1991) see the concept of need as offering the potential for a universal statement on social provision. They argue that there are two basic human needs that are required to ensure the 'avoidance of serious harm' (p. 50). The first basic need is *personal autonomy*, which they define as 'the ability to make informed choices about what should be done and how to go about doing it' (p. 53). The second basic need is *physical survival and health*, which is described as the ability to carry out necessary actions. The loss of either autonomy or health would entail disablement and an inability to lead anything near to a normal life, and this would apply regardless of time, culture or place. According to Doyal and Gough, these two basic needs are therefore universal.

In addition to these two basic needs, they suggest that there are a number of *universal satisfiers*, such as food, water, security and housing. These are derivative of the basic needs, in that they are required to maintain our autonomy and health and so ensure we avoid serious harm. However, whilst they are universal, the actual level required for satisfaction will differ according to time, place and culture: we all need housing to protect our autonomy and health, but what this amounts to in terms of space standards, building type, size, etc., is relative to a particular culture.

What is clear from Doyal and Gough's discussion is that a need is an imperative. If we are without this thing we need, the consequences may well be severe. It is not merely a case that we are disappointed that our aspirations have not been met and that we have had to choose something else in its place. If we do not have our needs met, we would be at risk of serious harm and our lives would be in danger. This means that our needs require immediate attention. We cannot ignore them or put off dealing with them for very long.

Doyal and Gough's (1991) formulation of universal needs carries with it the probability that individuals may be unaware of what some of their needs are, or rather, it is not necessary to be aware of needs to have them. Such needs will therefore have to be determined, to an extent at least, externally. Likewise, Bengtsson (1995), citing Culyer, gives one definition of need as 'one party's definition of what another should have' (p. 132). There is, then, an apparent consensus that a need can only be fully defined externally. However, according to Percy-Smith (1996), needs are capable of objective definition, measurement and assessment and can therefore form a legitimate basis for the state's action.

A more philosophical approach to defining need appears to substantiate this objective and external view. Wants and desires must be intentional states in that we must be aware of the condition (Griffin, 1986; Plant, 1991).

We purposefully want or desire something, and so Griffin (1986) sees that a want or desire is tied to our perception of an object. However, need is not an intentional verb. It does not have to be related to the perception of an object, nor to our particular experiences. We need something only because it is necessary, not because we crave or desire it. According to Griffin, we do not have to know we have a need for it to exist, whilst we must actively want or desire something. Needs exist regardless of our consciousness of them.

We might find Griffin's argument initially quite strange: how can we have a need and not know anything about it? However, a small child or an elderly person suffering from dementia would have no conception of the importance of avoiding serious harm or appreciate the significance of personal autonomy. A small child might not know that a busy road is dangerous and that they need to take care, and nor could they read the word 'poison' written in big letters on the bottle accidentally left within reach. But it is not just the very young and the old who may be unaware of their needs. We might not be aware that we are suffering from cancer until it is too late, and this is simply because we are unaware of the symptoms. Similarly, we might ignore some discomfort or misinterpret heart problems as heartburn. But our ignorance of the true state of our health is irrelevant to our situation: the cancer or heart problem is there and needs treating whether we currently know about it or not.

This is perhaps the most significant point when considering the assessment and fulfilment of need. If individuals are unaware of their needs, they must either be made aware or have the need met for them. Hence some societies have compulsory social insurance schemes to force people to save for the time when they are ill or elderly. Other states provide goods and services like health care and housing centrally, regardless of the ability to pay, so that there are no costs involved and no excuse not to deal with the discomfort.

However, this does not mean we have no choice with regard to need. Griffin (1986) suggests that there are two sorts of needs. First, there are *basic needs*, which we all have by virtue of being human. We can see these as being similar to those defined by Doyal and Gough. But, second, Griffin states we have what he terms *instrumental needs*, which occur because of the particular ends we choose. So, for example, we may choose to have a child, and this can quite properly be seen to be a voluntary action. However, once a woman is pregnant, she now has certain needs as a result, and once the child is born, the household has additional needs in terms of space, income and health care. Like having a child, many of the choices that we make are consequential, in that once we have made the choice we cannot rescind it, or at least not without equally serious consequences (we only need to consider the moral and psychological dilemma of abortion to see this).

This suggests that many of the needs we now have, have arisen because of the choices we made earlier, be it the relationships we have had, the jobs we have taken or the commitments we have made to others. This, as we shall see in our discussion on responsibility below, has important consequences for policy making. As an example, we might say that being without a dwelling carries with it the potential for serious harm. Therefore, we would hope that the household would be helped as a priority. But does it not matter how the household became homeless? What if it was due entirely to their own actions: they perhaps neglected to pay their rent and so were evicted. Should this affect the way in which we deal with them? In policy terms, there is a distinction between homelessness legislation in England, which retains a test of intentionality precisely to deal with deliberate and avoidable acts and omissions, and Scotland, where the intentionality clause has been abolished on the basis that what matters is dealing with homelessness and not apportioning blame. So English and Scottish legislators persist with different approaches to instrumental needs.

What this means is that, despite Levine's distinction between wants and needs, it is never possible to separate need from choice completely. Individuals have needs because of the choices they have made, and these needs do not go away merely because we see them as less serious than basic needs. This is particularly the case in developed economies where most people live well above a basic subsistence level. Many of the state's resources are not used to maintain basic needs but go well beyond this. Hospitals provide care to a high level and in countries like the UK it is possible to receive fertility treatment and some forms of cosmetic surgery via the National Health Service. However, most UK citizens would not see this as excessive or improper. It is rather the case that we are capable of successfully intervening and therefore we should. Indeed, current debates concerning health care in the UK tend to be about the lack of sufficient resources to fund certain identified needs, either because drugs are deemed too expensive or because different policies pertain in different parts of the country (again this relates to diverging policies between England and Scotland).

What is significant about this development, however, is that UK hospitals do not provide fertility treatment *instead* of basic care but *as well as*. Likewise, when social landlords fulfil the Decent Homes Standard, they cannot help but meet the very basic standards. Luxuries, as it were, sit on top of basic requirements, and so living in a mansion would see our basic needs fulfilled, as well as matching up with our aspirations.

This suggests that a discussion on need alone would be rather limiting. Of course, we want basic needs to be met, and this may serve as a sound justification for housing subsidies and state provision. However, it is not enough in itself. We want and expect to go beyond basic needs and would not be happy to return to a subsistence existence. Meeting need is important, but it is not enough. We want and expect to be able to choose and to have a civilised life that is determined by the current conditions in which we live. In other words, we want to make choices.

Think point   Dad of 15 gets wife and girlfriend pregnant

Read the following article taken from the AOL news site in 2006, and then answer the questions below.

The wife and girlfriend of an unemployed father of 15 who sparked a national outcry when he complained about the size of his council house are both pregnant, according to reports.

Mick Philpott, of Derby, claimed Britain was 'going down the pan' after his local council said it could not provide him with a bigger home for his huge clan. Now it has emerged that the 49-year-old is about to become a father to children numbers 16 and 17.

Wife Mairead and girlfriend Lisa Willis are both expecting, he told the *Derby Evening Telegraph*. It reports he vowed to have a vasectomy, saying that he was 'annoyed with himself'.

'It's just one of those things that they've both fallen pregnant,' he said.

Mr Philpott refused to comment on the report at his Victory Road home. He lives at the property with his 25-year-old wife, who is the mother of their five children, aged one to seven. Sharing their home is his 22-year-old girlfriend and their three young children. Miss Willis also has another child, aged six, from a previous relationship, who lives at the house. And Mr Philpott is father to another seven offspring from three previous relationships.

Source: http://news.aol.co.uk/dad-of-15-gets-
wife-and/article/20061115105009990001
(downloaded 15 November 2006)

1   Does Mr Philpott need a bigger council house?

2   How much of his predicament is due to choice?

3   Do the choices individuals make have any implications for whether we see them as being in need?

4   What does this case say about the connection between need and choice?

Choice

If need has traditionally been used to justify the provision of social housing, we could equally state that the modern twenty-first century buzzword is choice. Housing organisations in the Netherlands have long used choice-based lettings to allocate their dwellings. In England, the government has sought to extend choice through a range of policies from rent restructuring, Housing Benefit, and choice-based lettings (DETR, 2000). The government recognises that choice in housing lags behind other areas, 'As we enter this new millennium it is right that our policies should work towards giving people the choice they expect in other areas of life' (DETR, 2000, p. 5).

These policies can be seen as a means of empowering households. The aim is to redesignate applicants as customers who are empowered 'to make decisions on choosing housing which meets their requirements' (p. 78). One example of this attempt to empower households is the reforms to Housing Benefit, which involves paying the benefit to the claimant rather than their landlord (DWP, 2002). The government seems to want to alter the very expectations of applicants and to move towards a more equal relationship between landlord and tenant.

Kemp (1997, 2007b) has argued that there has been a general shift towards more consumer-oriented structures across the developed world. Countries such as the Netherlands, Australia and New Zealand have shifted towards demand side subsidies paid to households rather than to housing organisations. This is an important shift for a number of reasons. Not only does it seek to empower households and alter the relationship between landlord and tenant, it also implies a different function for housing subsidies and government involvement in housing. Subsidies paid to individuals assume that 'the housing problem' is a lack of income and access to housing, rather than a shortage of housing itself. Government intervention is geared towards ensuring households can compete in markets rather than encouraging new development.

So, shifting the emphasis away from need and towards choice is important in showing a change in the direction of policy that favours households instead of landlords. It suggests that we see social housing as being less important than it was in the past. It might also indicate that the role of experts who can make external judgements on the needs of others is being questioned. Instead we should place more emphasis on the ability of individuals to make decisions for themselves. This is a significant shift that, as we shall see, can have important consequences for individual outcomes. In particular, what if households, who are expected to make decisions themselves, prove to be incapable? What if they make a bad decision and end up homeless? Should we accept this? But we are perhaps getting ahead of ourselves. Before criticising choice, we need to determine just what it is and what it means for housing finance.

What do we mean by choice?

One of the problems when discussing choice in housing is that there has been all too little reflection on what is meant by the term. Like need, it is one of those concepts that we use all the time, and we assume we know what it means. Often it is seen almost as a quality which individuals carry within them, which can be released by the right sort of policy mechanism: individuals 'have choice' and all that is needed is the opportunity to exercise it.

However, this is too simplistic: the concept is rather a complex one that carries with it certain implications that have been underappreciated in the current debate on extending choice in housing. Choice, as we have just hinted, has important moral implications for both consumers and organisations. Indeed the allocation of social housing is itself a moral issue. As we have suggested, making a decision about allocating a government funded dwelling to one household rather than another is not a value neutral process. We need to have reasons for choosing one household and not the other. It may be because the household chosen is more deserving, or in greatest need. Likewise, when we decide to provide subsidies to households rather than landlords, we are making a judgement on the competence of individuals to decide for themselves, as well as implicitly commenting on the ability of landlords to act properly on their tenants' behalf.

Choice, in a moral sense, relates to notions of *autonomy*, *liberty* and *responsibility* (King, 2003). In this sense, a choice-based policy should be one that alters the power relations between landlord and tenant/applicant in favour of the latter. In turn, a greater burden is placed on applicants and tenants in terms of bearing the responsibility for their decisions. Hence it is entirely proper to connect choice with empowerment. What is at issue, therefore, is whether housing policies aimed at enhancing choice actually achieve this aim of empowerment.

Put simply, to have a choice or to choose suggests that we are able to *select from alternatives*, even if the alternative is an either/or between two less than perfect solutions. It further implies we are able to make a preference and thus distinguish between entities, and that we are able to proffer reasons for the choices we make. Choice is deemed to be a *capability* that individuals and households have, whereby they can materially affect their situation through the decisions they take. It is the point at which individuals take control over the decisions affecting them.

This raises what can be considered the most significant question in the debate over choice, namely, what is the level of knowledge that is presumed necessary in order to facilitate effective decision making? As Elster (1986, 1999) has shown, one of the essential prerequisites for rational choice is *information*. We need access to accurate and correct information before we can come to a considered decision.

According to Elster, in order 'for action to be rational it has to stand in specific relations to the desires, beliefs and information sets of the agent' (1999, p. 141). He argues that an understanding of rationality involves the interplay of these three levels of desires, beliefs and information sets.

First, for an action to be rational 'it has to be the best means of satisfying the desires of the agent, given his beliefs' (p. 142). There should be no better way of satisfying one's desires, otherwise the action is not rational. Second, Elster argues that the beliefs themselves should be rational, 'in the sense of being grounded in the information available to the agent' (p. 142). In particular, they will include beliefs about the opportunities available to the agent. However, Elster acknowledges that it might be the case that the agent is not aware of the full set of opportunities open to them. Thus they may be able to do more than they believe they can.

Connecting rationality to belief emphasises its subjective nature. Rational choice involves making some 'subjective estimate of the alternatives' (p. 143). This means that one can fail or be mistaken in the chosen action, without that action being irrational. According to Elster, an action is rational if 'one has no reason, after the fact, to think that one should have acted differently' (p. 144). Thus he argues that a drug addict may be said to be acting rationally if he or she is a person who subjectively discounts the future very heavily.

The third element of Elster's discussion of rational choice is the need for information. Elster suggests that there is a balance to be made in information gathering since we cannot make a rational decision without investing time and effort in doing so. Yet it might also be the case that gathering too much information is dangerous. We would hope a doctor does not wait too long to make a diagnosis, in case the patient dies. We should therefore seek some medium between considered diagnosis and decisive action, although Elster acknowledges that it might be difficult to locate where this point is.

What makes this balancing act more difficult, of course, is the asymmetrical nature of information (Hillier, 1997; Stiglitz, 2002). Private landlords may have more knowledge of market conditions and rent levels within a district, which would provide them with a significant advantage over applicants. The same asymmetrical relationship would apply in the social sector where the necessary information required for a choice-based letting system is filtered through the landlord's bureaucratic structures. Thus the costs of information gathering are determined by landlords.

Putting the three elements together leads Elster to state that rational choice is the principle that 'people make the most out of what they have' (1999, p. 145). This definition of rational choice is an important one. It recognises that rationality is a subjective notion and thus depends on desires and beliefs and information available to the decision maker. In doing so it recognises that individual decision makers do not start from positions of equality: 'what they have' will differ between individuals. This shows that the key issue is that of the resources available to the decision maker.

Elster's discussion shows that choice is always bounded by constraints. He sees these constraints as relating to the incentive structure within which the decision maker operates and the limited information that they may have. This notion is confirmed by Mulder (1996) in her work on housing choice in the Netherlands. She argues for a bounded rationality, whereby households only consider moving because of trigger events. Choice is not seen as a continuous event, but rather is contingent on certain key events, such as a job change, retirement or change in family circumstance. Households only see the need to choose as a necessary reaction to a trigger event. There is thus an important instrumental quality to choice, as well as to need: we choose because of the situation we are in and because we have to react. Furthermore, we choose *between* specific entities rather than having an inner quality that we might exercise as it suits us. We do not choose for its own sake but to achieve a particular effect.

Effective choice

Choice is meant to allow individuals to influence their own situation materially. The idea of choice-based policies is to allow individuals to make their lives better. The problem is that choice over public services cannot be made autonomously, but is in the gift of a bureaucracy determined to control it. Social landlords control the resources and the access to them, and this means that it is landlords who determine the level of choice applicants and tenants actually have. Likewise, those on low incomes need subsidies to be determined and controlled by government before they can make choices. Therefore we can suggest that the essence of choice is *control*.

If we are to make the most of what we have, it therefore matters *what* we have and *how much* we are able to make of it. One way of describing this is as *effective choice* (Brown and King, 2005; King, 1996). This can be defined as the ability of individuals to control their environment and gain access to the resources that translate choice into empowerment. Effective choice exists therefore when we are capable of controlling our environment, as opposed to having a merely abstract choice. Individuals with effective choice could be said to be empowered, and thus capable of making the most of what they have.

We can define three principles for housing processes based on effective choice. The first principle involves the *limitation* of the role and scale of government activity in housing. Central government does not need to set down distinct lines for action, but rather it should merely set limits or parameters within which agencies and individuals can operate. Thus government's role should be restricted to setting limits to action that allows for the maximum opportunity for individual fulfilment. Individuals can only choose if they are given the space to do so, and this has implications for financial mechanisms and who controls them.

Second, the *control* of the housing process should be local and in the hands of those who use the outcomes of the process. The smaller the scale, the better the outcomes can be manipulated by the users. This presupposes that choice-based systems should be 'bottom-up' and not determined by central government prescription. Third, control is activated by *access* to resources. Partly, of course, this is a function of income, but it also relates to the facilitation of resources and the means of accessing them at the requisite level.

These three principles of limits, control and access might be useful as a means of measuring the actual extent to which choice is truly present in housing, always bearing in mind that these principles are to be seen as ideals and their attainment will never be absolute. Limitation and control are always going to be conditioned by questions of degree, and the control over resources will always, to an extent, be competitive, if only on grounds of scarcity. So they operate within the realm of owner occupation, where property rules limit the role of government, as well as other agencies and individuals.

But what this notion of effective choice also suggests is that choice is not an intrinsic quality – it is not something we have within us – but is rather a condition determined by the constraints placed upon us and the level of resources at our disposal.

This leads to a final point to consider regarding choice, which is whether, how and when choice is appropriate. As we have seen, when we raise the issue of resources, it becomes clear that choices will be limited. But also we need to factor in just who it is that is likely to be making the choices. Middle class households with a steady income and savings in the bank are more capable of making choices and bearing the consequences of taking the wrong option than a low income household facing the prospect of homelessness. Similarly, the actual conditions in the local housing market are also important. If there is excess demand for private rented housing, and if social housing is scarce, then it might not really be appropriate to talk about choice. The only agents with choice in this situation are the landlords, in that they can decide who they want as tenants.

In any case, for choice to be real, there needs to be competition between suppliers. The customer needs to have a real and meaningful alternative. But in order for all customers to have a choice, there must be an oversupply of housing. In simple terms, the last household has to be able to choose from at least two options. It may be argued, however, that this is rather wasteful of scarce resources and that it would be better instead to plan and provide housing on the basis of need to allow for a high level of provision for all.

Competition will always lead to a situation of winners and losers. Some households will obtain exactly the housing they desire, whilst others will face a much more limited choice. Of course, virtually no one ever has an unlimited choice. We are always limited by our income, by the time we can afford to take and what is available. But the consequences of no choice or a poor choice might be quite considerable for some people, particularly those with low or no income of their own.

This raises the question of whether we are prepared to allow households to pay the consequences of poor decision making. If we are allowed to choose, there is always the possibility we will choose wrongly or badly. But is this acceptable in a welfare system aimed at protecting the vulnerable? If a household uses their housing allowance to buy alcohol and they are accordingly evicted, are we happy as a society to say that this is their fault and leave them to deal with the consequences? If we find that they used the rent money to pay a fuel bill, or buy a pair of school shoes for their child, would we take a different view? We shall return to these issues in the next section, but what is clear is that we need to appreciate that choices have consequences.

This means we have to be aware of the purpose of social housing and government subsidies. If housing finance exists to make housing more affordable and to allow individuals access to good quality housing, do we really want a system that allows some people to fail? Is the purpose of social provision to provide a safety net or is it a means of acculturation and education? Are we aiming to *improve* people by making them more responsible and capable, or are we more concerned to help them?

What this boils down to is the question of whether choice and welfare go together? This is, of course, a huge issue and providing an answer is beyond the scope of this discussion. However, what it shows is that choice might be problematic. This does not mean that we should not pursue it as a policy aim. After all, in most European countries, as well as Australia and the USA, most households rely on the owner occupied and private rental sectors, and so can be said to have some degree of choice over their housing. So, instead of rejecting choice as a policy imperative, we need to be aware that certain consequences may accrue when society expects individual households to take decisions for themselves.

Think point   Where's my new house?

Read the following case and then consider the questions below:

> Mr and Mrs Smith have a teenage son and currently live in a council house in Kingsville. However, they are now divorced and so wish to live apart. Mr Smith wants to be allocated a property by the council but has yet to receive one he considers suitable. Kingsville District Council have offered a one bed flat, but Mr Smith says he needs a two bed flat so his son can stay. Both Mr and Mrs Smith – who has custody of the boy – claim the council is being negligent and unsympathetic.
>
> (Source: Based on an *Inside Housing* article, 9 March 2001, p. 5. The names and place have been changed.)

- Who caused the situation?
- Who should sort it out?
- What are the limits of the landlord's responsibility?

Responsibility

If we make a decision, like Mr and Mrs Smith in the 'think point' above, does that mean we have to bear the consequences? We are not made aware of the circumstances of the divorce and it might be that Mr Smith had done nothing wrong and is now the unfortunate victim of his wife's duplicity and an unsympathetic bureaucracy. If this were the case, we might feel that Mr Smith deserves to be helped. But what if the divorce were his fault and he is now staying put in the family home to get the most out of the situation that he can? Would this lead us to take a different view of the situation?

Many people might argue that the reasons for a situation are an important consideration in determining what is to be done to remedy that situation and who should be held responsible for doing it. If someone has caused a problem, then they should be the ones charged with sorting it out. However, what if that person, even though they accept their culpability, has no income or resources to sort out the mess? We have already come across this situation in this chapter when we discussed the difference between homelessness law in England and Scotland. The English believe there should be a test of intentionality to judge whether a household is to be helped, whilst the Scots take the view that what matters is that a person is destitute and in need of assistance.

One of the arguments against the Scottish position is that ignoring the cause of homelessness may actually encourage actions that themselves will lead to homelessness. If a tenant knows that they will be rehoused if they are evicted, why should they pay their rent? In England, however, it might be the case that eviction due to rent arrears is seen as an unreasonable omission on the part of the tenant and so they will not be rehoused. The intentionality clause remains in England precisely to deter what policy makers see as unreasonable acts on the part of tenants.

This brief discussion on homelessness raises the core elements of any discussion on responsibility. The English view might be portrayed as placing the notion of *blame* at the centre of policy making. In Scotland, what is more important is who is capable of sorting out the problem, or who is *tasked* with clearing up the mess. This dichotomy between blame and task is central to what follows.

Being responsible is where we are taken to be the primary cause of a particular situation. We are responsible because the situation would not have arisen but for our actions or omissions. This is to link responsibility with *causality*, in that we have to take upon ourselves certain tasks and actions as a result of past actions. This notion of responsibility is backward-looking since it is how the situation has arisen that is considered important. As a result of this causality we are deemed to be the person (or agency) who is tasked with sorting the issue out: 'you caused it, so you sort it out'.

Goodin (1998) suggests that we should separate out cause and task. We can be held to be to blame for a particular situation we have caused to come about, or we can be seen as the one tasked with its solution. It may well be that the fact that we are blamed will lead to us being tasked with its solution, but this need not be the case. What ought to matter, Goodin argues, is *who is able to sort it out rather than who caused it*.

Goodin argues that blame responsibility is backward-looking, and 'should be shunned for policy purposes but which nonetheless seems to dominate discussions of social welfare' (1998, p. 150). This form of responsibility seeks to praise or blame people for what they have done in the past, even if the aim is to shape future behaviour. He favours task responsibility precisely because it is forward-looking, in that it specifies 'whose job it is to see to it that certain tasks are performed and that certain things are accomplished' (p. 150). Goodin admits that there will be a 'shadow of the past' even here, in that we might want to look at how a situation came about in order to allocate tasks. However, according to Goodin, this should be seen merely as 'a further consequence rather than the principal substance' (p. 151) of responsibility. What Goodin is saying is that, whilst a person might not be completely exonerated of blame, what matters is not who caused it but who can sort it out.

Goodin's reasoning for championing task responsibility is that history is not easily reversible and that 'people cannot always get themselves out of the jam as easily as they got themselves into it' (p. 152). He goes on:

> Sometimes others are better situated to get them out of a jam that they and they alone got themselves into. In such circumstances, who 'caused' the problem (whom to assign backward-looking 'blame responsibility' for it) is one thing. Who can best remedy it (whom to assign forward-looking 'task responsibility' for it) is another thing altogether.
>
> (Goodin, 1998, p. 152)

Thus we may be homeless because we have omitted to make regular rent payments, and so we can be held to blame for this, but it does not mean that we are able to remedy the omission. Some other person or agency might be better placed to remedy this situation and thus be tasked with finding housing for us.

As Goodin himself recognises, this is a contentious argument, in that it might be supposed that, in some situations, the person responsible could be determined merely on the basis of relative resources, rather than on any moral basis at all. What is important to Goodin, however, is the empirical or instrumental quality of welfare: if we assert that a particular level of welfare or flourishing is desirable or even necessary, we should then be primarily concerned with achieving those outcomes; hence the concern to look forward rather than back. Accordingly, he argues that smokers 'have only themselves to blame for their cancers' (p. 153). But once they have cancer, there is 'nothing further that they could do to cure themselves of it' (p. 153).

On one level Goodin's point is correct, in that what is important in cancer treatment is not why the cancer is there and who is to blame, but how and whether it can be treated. We are more concerned with cure than cause. However, there is still a problem with Goodin's argument. He is prepared to admit that there is 'a shadow of the past' looming over the apportioning of tasks. However, apart from this, he suggests that blame and task are entirely separate. This may be the case, but that does not imply that we should adopt one view at the expense of the other. We may not be able to treat our own cancer, but we can still be blamed for it and held to account as well. We can argue that certain forms of treatment should be seen as imperatives for which the state will pay, whilst others are to be met through private insurance. Thus we could exclude certain treatments from state-run health care systems and force individuals to insure themselves against them. Likewise, private insurance companies or even social insurance systems might choose to charge some customers more because of their behaviour. Smokers, for instance, pay higher life insurance premiums and young men, who are more likely to be involved in road traffic accidents, pay more for car insurance. This does not mean that the insurance companies are shirking their 'task responsibility' if there is a cancer or a car accident. Rather it means that the risk is altered as a result of the actions of the customer, and it is felt to be acceptable that this risk be accounted for. In this sense the insurance company is quite legitimately incorporating the 'shadow of the past' into its deliberations. This is precisely because the shadow is deemed to be cast into the future and will materially affect the relation between the company and its clients.

We need also to be aware that *not* apportioning blame is a substantive issue in itself. By openly stating that we will not apportion blame, we might alter behaviour for the worse. As we have stated already, why should anyone act responsibly if they know that they will not be held to account for it? If this view is correct, it does matter who is held responsible and what is expected of them.

In the light of this concern, one way of discussing the notion of responsibility is whether it is internalised or externalised. Schmidtz (1998) suggests that responsibility is externalised 'when people do not take responsibility: for messes they cause, for messes in which they find themselves' and when 'people regard the cleanup as someone else's problem' (p. 8). This is precisely when we do not apportion blame, but instead state that responsibility should be located with an agency with the resources to solve it. The responsibility is therefore vested outside of the individual who caused the problem.

On the other hand, Schmidtz states that responsibility 'is internalised when agents take responsibility: for their welfare, for their futures, for the consequences of their actions' (p. 8). Like Goodin (1998), Schmidtz does not seek to relate responsibility to blame, seeing the issue as one of welfare or 'what makes people better off'. He argues that internalised responsibility is precisely what makes people better off, whilst externalising responsibility creates dependency and poverty: 'What strikes me about citizens of prosperous societies, then, is not their individualism so much as their willingness to take responsibility' (p. 9).

Schmidtz makes the point that if we are not taken to be responsible, then this means that the responsibility lies with some other person or agency instead. Whilst it may be that we are not held completely at fault for causing the situation, it is still perverse to pass that responsibility on to society, 'that is, people who are not even partly at fault' (p. 11). In the case of homelessness in Scotland, it might be argued that it is somewhat odd to make innocent taxpayers responsible for the messes caused by rent defaulters.

This leads Schmidtz to argue that 'what is woven into the welfare state is literally a pattern of transfer, not a pattern of sharing' (p. 75). Institutionalised welfare, as Nozick (1974) has argued, benefits some people at the expense of others. Exonerating people from blame for their situation, in this sense, does not help make them responsible, but then neither does passing the task on to those not to blame make *them* properly responsible. What happens is that individuals do not feel any sense of responsibility for their situation. But then, because the state undertakes to fulfil their welfare needs, individual taxpayers need feel no connection or sense of solidarity with those being assisted. Indeed they might even come to resent the state using 'their' money to support people with whom they feel they have little in common.

Schmidtz suggests that responsibility becomes externalised because the role of institutions is seen as the alleviation of immediate problems rather than internalising responsibility. Schmidtz sees the problem as a 'static perspective' (p. 21) in which only outcomes are considered. Instead, institutions should be concerned with the processes that individuals can use to fend for themselves. He suggests that 'property rights are pre-eminent among institutions that lead people to take responsibility for their welfare' (p. 22). He goes so far as to suggest that 'institutions of property (are) the human race's most pervasive and most successful experiment in internalised responsibility' (p. 25). What internalises responsibility more effectively than anything else is the attribution of property rights to individuals (we shall return to the issue of property rights when we discuss markets in chapter 3).

This is a controversial argument, but it is one that has recently had some resonance with policy makers. In particular, we have seen attempts to reform welfare in the USA to introduce a degree of conditionality so that benefit recipients only receive money by undertaking training or community work that prepares them for employment (Hirst, 2007; Rogers, 1999). The idea behind these reforms is that structures of provision should be geared towards changing the behaviour of individuals rather than merely keeping them on benefit. Benefit recipients should be forced to be active in their search for work rather than passively accepting welfare. This, as Schmidtz suggests, is a structural problem in terms of how welfare systems are organised.

More fundamentally it opens up our discussion to the role of markets and the state. Markets are places where property rights are traded. States are the only agents within a territory who can make claim to a portion of their citizens' property, on the basis that they require to use it for necessary services, which may include welfare provision. We therefore turn to look at the relationship between markets and government.

Think point Nobby

Read this case and consider the questions below:

There is a bus shelter on the Oundle Road in Peterborough which became the home for a homeless man known as Nobby. He was a bad-tempered man who refused to say what his real name was or where he came from. He lived with all his possessions in the bus shelter and refused to leave. Initially he was resented by the local residents, but in time he became accepted and the neighbours would provide him with food, old clothes and so on. Indeed when the local authority tried to move him on the local residents objected and stood up for Nobby's right to stay there. Indeed he refused to be housed by the local authority or to accept help from social services.

- Should Nobby be able to choose to live like this?
- Who would be responsible if he came to harm or died of exposure?
- Have the authorities fulfilled their responsibilities?

Conclusions

This has been a rather abstract chapter, with very little directly on housing finance. Yet this discussion has provided the necessary background for understanding the role of markets and the state in providing housing and hence the way that finance is used. It is these three concepts of need, choice and responsibility that are at the heart of the political economy of housing finance, in that they provide justification for public action and place limits on private action. We can therefore move on from here to more practical matters.

Further reading

There is a considerable literature on these issues and much of it can be quite demanding. A book that covers all of these issues in detail and relates them to housing is *A Social Philosophy of Housing* (King, 2003). I also discuss need at some length in my book, *Housing, Individuals and the State* (1998). In terms of choice a good starting point is the work of Jon Elster, particularly the introduction to his edited volume, *Rational Choice* (1986). A discussion on choice that relates to housing is offered by Brown and King's paper, 'The Power to Choose: Effective Choice and Housing Policy' (2005). As for responsibility, a good starting point is Schmidtz and Goodin (1998) who provide a debate between collectivist and individualist positions.

3

The importance of markets

- What markets are.
- The importance of prices and property rights in a market economy.
- Why housing is amenable to market provision.
- The nature of housing markets.
- The problem of market failure.

Introduction

When I was16 years old, I had a Saturday job working on Mr Bowring's fruit and vegetable stall on Peterborough market. I worked from six in the morning until six at night and all for £4.50. After I got used to the early start and the long day, I came to enjoy the noise and bustle of the market, with its bright colours and the smells of fruit and vegetables. I liked it best when it was not too busy, so I could chat with the girls on the sweet stall next to us, go for a walk and look at what was going on. Mr Bowring, however, liked it when it was busy, with lots of customers waiting to be served, and he would constantly be telling me to pay attention, to concentrate and not to turn my back on the customers.

The great thing about the market was the proximity of everything. The stalls were arranged in rows and we could see several other fruit and vegetable stalls near to us.

Mr Bowring would often take a walk to see what the other stallholders had got: were they charging more or less than him? Had they got anything different? Were the queues bigger around his competitors? Sometimes he would come back and put the price of apples up by a penny a pound (still in imperial in those days) or the price of bananas down a bit.

Mr Bowring didn't believe in shouting, but he was the exception. Most of the other stallholders would call out, advertising their special offers and their cheap prices, trying to attract customers. And so the day was filled with the shouting of others, becoming both more tired and more desperate as the day went on. Missing a customer was like committing a crime – hence Mr Bowring's constant chiding – in that the customer would now go off and spend their money somewhere else. For Mr Bowring, each apple, orange or pear was converted into its monetary value and treated lovingly, at least until they had been bagged up and sold.

In the middle of the afternoon, around 3 o'clock, things changed. The market became quieter and seemed to be more relaxed, with fewer people around and a slower pace. But now the shouts changed: the prices dropped, and the stallholders started with their special offers. Mr Bowring would keep quiet, but off he would go again, seeing what others were up to. He would come back with more changes, dropping the price, offering three for the price of two or something like that. Some of the fruit on the stall would not last until the next market day – Tuesday – and so Mr B wanted to receive something for it, to at least cover his costs. But then he was only doing what all the other stallholders were doing. And everyone knew each other and the competition was friendly and civilised, even if the language was sometimes as colourful as the awnings above the stalls.

And the clientele changed too. Late in the afternoon would come the bargain hunters, picking over the bananas, noticing that they might not be best quality and wanting to haggle about the price. This was fine with Mr B – but only he could do the haggling, and only then if he took a liking to the person. These latecomers wanted a bargain, perhaps because their income was limited, or just because they didn't want to pay the full price. Of course they had less choice – some of the stallholders had packed up early and some of the best produce had gone. But not Mr B, who would stay to the very end in the hope of picking up the last customer.

This type of environment – the traditional market with lots of stalls, many selling the same sorts of things – is competition at its simplest. It can be seen as the ideal of a market: there are many sellers and lots of potential buyers, all milling around and able to see what is on offer and at what price.

In this chapter we shall look at how markets work. We shall consider markets in general and then, of course, look at housing markets in particular. We shall define what markets are and what they aim to do. In particular, we shall look at two defining characteristics of markets, namely, prices and property rights. We shall then discuss some of the key characteristics of housing, which makes it amenable to a market-based system. We need to understand why markets play such a full role in housing provision, especially in comparison with other so-called welfare goods. But we also need to consider how housing markets actually do work and how they might fail to live up to the ideal of a market we have begun with. This will lead us to look at the role of the state and why governments have intervened in housing.

Consistent with the political approach taken in this book, we shall be dealing with markets in a conceptual manner rather than a more typical or traditional approach. Many discussions of housing markets, for example Maclennan (1982) and Oxley (2004), make use of supply and demand graphs and equations to progress their argument. The key problem with this approach is that graphical representations tend to show economic phenomena as being static and separate. What I wish to emphasise, as I stated in chapter 1, is the dynamic and interconnected nature of housing markets. This, I would argue, is best done through a political economy approach that stresses conceptual analysis rather than the methods of traditional economics.

What are markets?

A market can be seen as a physical entity, a place like Peterborough market where buyers and sellers come together within a defined space to buy and sell goods. This is the simple ideal of a market: where there are a number of traders competing against each other and so allowing customers to come to an informed decision on price and quantity. The customers are capable of making comparisons between each trader in terms of the price and quality of goods. But, of course, each trader too is equally capable of seeing what their competitors are offering and can change their behaviour accordingly.

This ideal of a market supposes that certain conditions exist and these are summarised in Table 3.1.

Table 3.1 Conditions for perfect competition

Perfect information.

Many buyers and sellers.

Individuals are rational actors who seek to maximise their outcomes.

No barriers to entry in the market.

First, there is the assumption that both consumers and suppliers have perfect information about the market. They either have, or can easily obtain, all the information on price and quantity in the market. Second, there are many suppliers so that no one person or group has market power and is therefore able to control the price. Mr Bowring had to alter his prices to take account of his competitors, or at least he had to if he wished to sell anything because it was all too easy for customers to spend 20 minutes walking around the entire market. Third, it is assumed that the various players act rationally. It is held that suppliers seek to maximise their profits and consumers to maximise their utility, or the amount of benefit for any given amount of money spent. This means that all parties alter their behaviour according to market conditions: suppliers will supply more when prices rise and less when they fall; consumers will demand more as prices fall and less as they rise. Finally, there are no barriers to entry to the market. This means that it is straightforward for any person to set up in business, and no one who has the money is prevented from buying the goods should they wish.

But whilst it is convenient to use a place like Peterborough market as the perfect example, it is by no means the case that all markets are like this. This means that some of the assumptions discussed above might not always hold good. In particular, it is now quite rare for a market to be contiguous and exist in one defined place. Most markets, particularly when we talk about housing markets, are not within a physically confined space where we can compare one supplier with another.

For example, we might now buy our apples from a supermarket instead of a street market, and we certainly do not drive from Tesco to Morrison's to Sainsbury's and then on to Waitrose to compare prices. Instead we might well stay with the one supermarket that we know offers the range and quality of produce we want. Yet, if it fails to do this and its prices no longer stand comparison with its competitors, we will change to another supermarket. Indeed, there were many regular customers who would walk straight past other stalls to buy their fruit and vegetables from Mr Bowring's stall. But we knew that they only did so because they were certain that they would get what they wanted and in any case could readily go elsewhere.

But it is no longer even necessary to leave the house to participate in a market. The development of Internet shopping and sites like eBay mean that markets need not be physical spaces at all. We can purchase our groceries online and have them delivered, and we can compare the price of the latest Harry Potter novel on the various online booksellers' websites and make a choice accordingly.

So, instead of seeing markets as physical spaces, they are best seen as a set of relations between people and companies and other organisations.

Indeed markets are an example of human interaction. It is merely a convenient way of describing 'a set of transactions by which money and goods change hands' (Levine, 1995, p. 48). It is where buyers and sellers come together to meet their needs to the best of their advantage. Hence eBay is just as good an example as Peterborough market.

We tend to talk about 'the market', but this is usually where we wish to make a political point, or to contrast it with government. In this way, the term is often taken as either a criticism or as a totem. 'The market' is either what impoverishes the developing world and is organised for the benefit of the filthy rich, or it is seen as an ideal form of social organisation and the means of liberating individuals from the dead hand of government intervention. But in either case there is a tendency to preface the word market with the definite article 'the' as if it is just one, albeit very large, thing.

But it is not really proper to talk in this manner. As Levine (1995) states, a market can refer to all transactions – hence national and even global markets – or the term can be used for a specific subset of all transactions, such as the labour market or the housing market. But these subsets can and should be divided further. So we can talk of regional or local housing markets, or particular types of housing market, such as private renting in Kensington or owner occupation in Wigan. Even within these subdivisions we might be able to break them down further, as households in Wigan want particular types of property in specific parts of the town. So we can talk of the markets for three bedroom houses and for one bedroom apartments, which effectively have different customers and which may be affected by different factors, such that prices in one offer no real guide to prices in the other.

So in terms of a definition of a market we should not see it necessarily as a physical place and nor is it just one thing. Taking these issues into account, we can concur with O'Neill, who states that a market economy can be defined as:

> those social and institutional arrangements through which goods are regularly produced for, distributed by and subject to contractual forms of exchange in which money and property rights over goods are transferred between agents.
>
> (O'Neill, 1998, p. 4)

This definition does not depend on any particular place or sense of a contiguous entity. Rather it can enclose a global economy where goods and services are traded internationally, as well as the local market for one bedroom apartments in Wigan. There are a number of elements of O'Neill's definition that we need to stress. First, a market is a social entity. It is a set of relations between households and businesses where different needs and desires are matched. Second, O'Neill stresses the institutional nature of markets. This does not refer to a physical place, but rather relates to the crucial point that markets need formal social, legal and political arrangements to underpin them. Markets only operate when there is a means of enforcing rights and contracts on each party to a transaction. Buyers and sellers need to be able to trust each other and to have a degree of certainty that the other party will deliver what they have committed to. This shows that the political use of the term 'market' that places it in opposition to government intervention is somewhat simplistic. As Oxley (2004) has suggested, markets need a legal and political framework in which to operate, and this would apply even in the most liberal of market-based societies.

Markets therefore are a social arrangement that exists to allocate goods and services and the rights over them. The reason that such an arrangement is necessary is because there are never enough goods and services to go around and thus some form of mechanism is needed to allocate them. The crucial point therefore is that of *scarcity*: if there is a limited number of goods and services, which may have competing uses, there needs to be some reliable means for determining their most effective use.

Of course, this does not mean that allocations have to be made by markets, but merely that this is one of the main means by which it can be, and has been, done. Allocations can be made by central planning or by a dictator, but decisions will still need to be taken. The argument of proponents of markets, such as Hayek (1960, 1988), is that markets are the most efficient form of social arrangement for the allocation of scarce goods and services.

Table 3.2   The functions of markets

- They are a means of allocating scarce resources. If resources will always be relatively scarce, some means of distributing them is needed. In markets this is done through the price mechanism, which determines the relative scarcity of goods and services.

- A market is a means of matching wants and needs at the lowest price and through the most efficient means. This is because markets encourage competition between suppliers who are forced to reduce their prices – and hence their costs – to win a share of customers.

- Markets allow individual customers to make choices. An individual customer is not forced to purchase anything, but rather they are able to choose between a range of goods, depending on how much money they have available and what their priorities are.

On the basis of this discussion we can point to a number of functions that markets perform, which are highlighted in Table 3.2. We can see markets, therefore, as being about information gathering and decision making: it allows us to gather the necessary information to make an informed decision about meeting our needs and desires.

Indeed, contrary to the ideal of perfect competition, the actual information required to make a market decision is rather simple: *how much is it?* As customers, we do not need to know how apples are grown or how they reach the market stall. All we need to be aware of is the price of apples and whether we can afford them. What this points to is the importance of price as the key signal of information in a market.

Prices

The importance of prices is that they provide the organising mechanism within markets. Sowell (2007) states that markets are not centrally co-ordinated and there is no individual or agency that controls them. But this:

> does not mean that these things just happen randomly or chaotically. Each consumer, producer, retailer, landlord, or worker makes individual transactions with other individuals on whatever terms are mutually agreeable. Prices convey these terms, not just to the particular individuals immediately involved but throughout the whole economic system – and indeed, throughout the world.
>
> (Sowell, 2007, pp. 12–13)

Price is essentially a means of signalling information to individuals and businesses about what is available and whether it is attainable. The key here is the relationship between price and scarcity. Sowell suggests that 'Many people see prices as simply obstacles to their getting the things they want' (p. 13), and so those seeking a beach-front house might abandon such a plan when they realise the price is beyond their reach. Therefore, for them, if the price were lower, perhaps due to government regulation or direct provision, they would have been able to gain their desire. But this is to get things the wrong way round. As Sowell states:

> high prices are not the reason we cannot all live on the beach front. On the contrary, the inherent reality is that there are not nearly enough beach-front homes to go around and prices simply convey that underlying reality. When many people bid for a relatively few homes, those homes become very expensive because of supply and demand. But it is not prices

that cause the scarcity, which would exist under whatever other kind of economic system or social arrangements might be used instead. There would be the same scarcity under feudalism or socialism or in a tribal society.

(Sowell, 2007, p. 14)

If it were not price that controlled access to these scarce dwellings, it would have to be something else, such as 'bureaucratic fiat, political favouritism or random chance' (p. 14). The real problem is that there are simply not enough houses of the right sort available for all those who would want one, and so there has to be some means of allocating them. In a market system this is done by price. So for Sowell, 'Prices are like messengers conveying news' (p. 14), and sometimes this news will be bad, in that the price will put the beach-front house out of the reach of all but the wealthy. The price, though, is not the cause of the problem but rather the means by which the nature of that problem is discovered.

Once this information has been discovered, it allows individuals and businesses to take decisions. We can state that prices provide 'incentives to affect behaviour in the use of resources and their resulting products' (Sowell, 2007, p. 15). Hence, once we discover the price of a beach-front house we alter our aspirations and look for housing within our price range. But, of course, should the price of such dwellings fall, we might come back to the market.

The virtue of the price mechanism as an organising principle can be shown by contrasting it with central planning like that of the former Soviet Union, where bureaucrats set prices by fiat. The problem for the Soviets was that they had to keep track of over 24 million separate prices. Sowell argues that a society of 100 million people can keep track of these prices far more easily, and this is because 'no given individual or business enterprise has to keep track of more than the relatively few prices that are relevant to their decision-making' (p. 17). As individuals with specific needs and the ability to make choices over the things that are close to us, we do not need to know the price of everything. We only need to know the price of those things we wish to buy, and we can readily come into contact with this information every time we journey to the supermarket or fill up our car with petrol.

But the problem for the bureaucrat is not merely one of keeping track of the prices of lots of things. If this were so, it would be possible to improve price planning merely by employing more bureaucrats. However, the issue is not just one of changing prices, but the fact that prices change *relative* to each other: so, for example, increased demand for steel for building will raise its price, but this will also raise the price for all those other services that depend on steel, for example, cutlery and shipbuilding. Hence we need to know what effect a change in price of one good will have on another. This is because scarce resources can have multiple uses – steel can be used to make both knives and ships – and also because it might be possible to substitute one good for another. So were steel to become more expensive, we might decide to build using other forms of construction, such as traditional brick or concrete.

In any case, society as a whole always has to pay the full cost of things, regardless of whether the full price is charged to individuals. If prices are not used, rationing has to take another form: but it does not disappear any more than the full costs do. The full cost of a thing does not go away; it is merely borne by someone else.

The key to understanding the role of prices, therefore, is the amount of knowledge that is required. Sowell argues that:

> Knowledge is one of the most scarce of all resources and a pricing system economizes on its use by forcing those with the most knowledge of their own particular situation to make bids for goods and resources based on that knowledge, rather than on their ability to influence other people in planning commissions, legislatures, or royal palaces.
>
> (Sowell, 2007, p. 27)

In a market we do not need to have perfect information because we do not require any information on goods that do not interest us; rather, what matters are the prices of the things we want to buy, and 'Price fluctuations are a way of letting a little knowledge go a long way' (Sowell, 2007, p. 32).

This specific relation we have with the prices of things is important, in that it helps explain how markets are able to operate. We tend to think that prices are an objective measure of the value of something: if a house costs £200,000, then that is its objective value. After all, no one individual can alter that price merely by an act of will or just because they think it is too much. Rather, all we can do if we cannot afford it or think it too much is to go away and buy something else.

But this does not mean that prices are set by any objective measure. Rather, prices are based on subjective values, in that any transaction must involve each party believing they are better off as a result of that transaction. So to continue with the example of the £200,000 house, one party must value the house at more than £200,000, otherwise they would keep their money and not purchase the house. However, the other party to the transaction must value the £200,000 more than the house. If this were not so, the transaction could not take place. This means that there can be no such thing as 'objective' value. Indeed, transactions only occur because we value things differently and therefore the price signals a different subjective response in each party.

As is becoming clear, the interaction of prices is complex. A market economy depends on what Sowell terms *systemic causation*: this involves 'complex reciprocal interactions' (2007, p. 63). This is when the behaviour of one element alters another and is in turn altered by it. It is not then the case that there is a simple linear interaction, as when one snooker ball hits another. Rather, there is reciprocity in the interaction, such that all elements behave differently; there is no straightforward causality.

This means that we have to be concerned with what *emerges* rather than what was intended. It also means that the impact of any one decision is small and ineffectual. It is the combination of all these decisions that has the real impact. This means that decisions cannot be taken on a whim or by a sustained act of will: all decisions are consequential to the individual but not necessarily to the market or to others.

The idea of intentions has a long history in political economy and it is worth looking at this briefly as this will shed some light on the issue of knowledge and the role that prices play in markets. Hayek (1978) is concerned with the nature of decision making in a complex modern society. He makes the distinction between two types of rationalism, which he calls *constructivist* and *evolutionary*. Constructivist rationalists believe that all human institutions and behaviour are the result of human reason and human will. Human beings can therefore master society and come to control and reform it. It is the belief that human institutions can be constructed to achieve particular desired aims. This is the mentality of the central planner trying to set all the prices in an economy. Hayek contrasts this with evolutionary rationalism, which is an attempt to understand how civilisation has developed, but with the attendant recognition of the limits of our current knowledge and thus the likelihood of unintended and unforeseen consequences. According to Hayek, evolutionary rationalism assumes that knowledge accumulates through individual action and experience, but in an unpredictable way. This implies that social change is better seen as a slow development caused by an untold number of actions, and not as the result of deliberate acts of manipulation.

Accordingly, Hayek (1948, 1967) suggests that social evolution, including the development of markets, occurs through human action, but not human design. Here he is concerned to correct what he considers to be the fallacy of constructivist rationalism which, he suggests, pervades collectivist approaches to social and public policy (Hayek (1967, 1978, 1988). This is the belief within collectivist approaches that, as all institutions have been made by human action, they can be remade by further deliberate action. This, according to Hayek, is a fundamental error on the part of policy makers. Institutions have developed in a particular way out of the uncoordinated inter-relationship of millions of individual actions, none of which in themselves were of fundamental significance. This is a similar point to that made by Sowell (2007) when he states that no one individual is capable of altering the prices, yet markets are merely the combination of millions of individual decisions in reaction to price.

Hayek's argument is based on what is one of the founding concepts of market analysis: the metaphor of *the invisible hand*. This term was first explicitly formulated by Adam Smith in the eighteenth century. He used the term to suggest a socially beneficent outcome from self-interested actions. He saw that markets were not centrally co-ordinated but were rather the accumulation of individual actions by individual consumers and producers, each seeking to maximise their outcomes. Beneficial outcomes were arranged *as if by an invisible hand*. We should note that Smith was not suggesting that the invisible hand was an actual thing: it is metaphor for how a market works for the benefit of a society, without any central direction and without any one individual intending to meet any needs but his or her own.

However, the metaphor has now become widened, so that an invisible hand explanation could now be defined as identifying 'any argument that proposes to show how some regular phenomenon emerged or could have emerged "spontaneously" or "unintendedly" from the actions of many persons' (Koppl, 1994, p. 192). It is where many individuals (and institutions) following their own interests arrive at an outcome that none of them would have intended. It is where the pattern that emerges is not that predicted by any of the individual players when deciding what actions would best suit their purposes.

This idea of the invisible hand provides a very sophisticated model for how an economy operates. In particular, it allows us to see that market outcomes are essentially the result of unintended consequences and the crossover effects of decision makers operating with only limited knowledge, namely the price of things. It tells us that markets have not developed as a result of specific policies or government action, but rather as the result of countless individual decisions over centuries. Each of these decisions was of little consequence, but each has some impact in determining the subsequent

Think point

Make a list of the main qualities of a street market. Now apply these qualities to the buying and selling of housing.

How similar is the housing market to a street market?

actions of others. This issue of unintended consequences is one that we shall return to in the next chapter and in chapter 5. But for now it shows that markets are hugely complex. Yet this complexity is itself based on the simple notion of prices determining individual actions within a market.

Property rights

Markets work on the basis of trade at a particular price but, in order to trade something, you have to have rights over it. In other words, you must own it. Therefore we can suggest that the basis of any market relationship is property ownership. If we return to O'Neill's definition of a market economy we see that he conceives of a market as being concerned with 'contractual forms of exchange in which money and property rights over goods are transferred between agents' (1998, p. 4). We pay for things using money, but this means that the right to a thing – its ownership – is now transferred over to us. We therefore need to understand property rights if we are to gain a full picture of markets.

But there is another reason why we should be interested in property rights, namely, that much of the housing finance used in the world is to allow for the transfer of property rights. We borrow money to buy a house. What this effectively means is that we purchase the rights over that asset. We also purchase rights over a dwelling through payment of rent and so we need to remember that a tenancy also involves the granting of property rights. For most people, therefore, their housing is likely to be the most significant form of property ownership.

When we say we own something what does this mean? Just what are property rights? Essentially it involves three things. First, to say we own something means we have the right to *use* it. It is legitimately at our disposal and we can determine what is done with it.[1] The second element follows on from this: I have the right to *exclusive* use. It is for me to decide who may use it and, if I wish, I can quite properly prevent all others from having access to it. My rights are therefore backed by some form of protection that allows for the exclusion of unwanted others. The third element – and this is what separates owning a house from renting one – is the right to dispose of or transfer the item as I see fit. As it is mine, I may dispose of it (although I may have to do this responsibly and within defined limits: I may sell my house, but not refuse to sell it to a particular individual on the basis of their ethnicity, for instance, and nor can I dispose of it by burning it down). I can sell the property for as much as I can get or I can give it away; I can transfer part or all of the property to another (perhaps to my wife or children for tax reasons) and I can leave it to whom I wish.

Therefore to say we own something means we have the exclusive use of it and the right to transfer it to another. So when we carry out a transaction in a market we transfer our rights of exclusive use and disposal over something (which may be money) in return for gaining rights over something else.

Property rights are therefore a necessary element of any market-based system. Indeed the notion of property rights has figured very significantly in modern social and economic thinking, and I wish to look at three particular views on property rights in some more detail. My reason for doing this is because it will, in turn, shed light on the legitimate role of markets and the state, in that the extent and limits of property rights are at the heart of debates about the role that the state has in influencing and controlling markets: a market society depends on property ownership, and so the important issue is how far we wish to protect property rights and thus allow markets to operate properly. This discussion will therefore help to set up the discussion in the later chapters of this book, which will look at how markets and the state interact with regard to housing finance.

The three views I wish to explore are different, yet all significant in their own way: one is a libertarian view that links individual rights to markets and shows some close similarity to the views on the invisible hand we discussed above; the second is a conservative position that more closely links ownership to the development of social relations; and the third view shows the connection of property rights to economic development, which has become influential in discussing why capitalism works in some parts of the world but not in others.

Entitlement

One of the most influential works of political philosophy of the last 40 years is Robert Nozick's *Anarchy, State and Utopia* (1974). This is a controversial, difficult, but brilliant discussion of what might be called *natural rights libertarianism*. This is the belief that humans have natural rights and that this justifies maximising individual freedom above all else. For Nozick, individual freedom is more important than equality, social justice, meeting needs or any other principle.

So Nozick's starting point is the inviolability of individual rights. Accordingly, he states that 'Individuals have rights, and there are things no person or group may do to them (without violating their rights)' (1974, p. ix). This limits what others may do to, and for, a person without infringing their rights.

Nozick's position is typical of most libertarians, be they on the left or right, in that he bases his position on the self-ownership of persons. We have ownership over our own self and our bodies and this means that others have no rights to control us. According to Vallentyne (2000), 'agents own themselves in just the same way that they can fully own inanimate objects' (p. 2). Individual agents have property rights over themselves and thus have rights of control and transfer.

This position leads Nozick to assert that there is no notion of the public or social good, merely benefits and disbenefits that might accrue to individuals. The actions of the state have the effect of benefiting some individuals by adding to their property, but this is arrived at through forcibly removing the property of others. Hence he states:

> there is no *social entity* with a good that undergoes some sacrifice for its own good. There are only individual people, different individual people, with their own individual lives. Using one of these people for the benefit of others, uses him and benefits the others. Nothing more. What happens is that something is done to him for the sake of others. Talk of an overall social good covers this up. (Intentionally?) To use a person in this way does not sufficiently respect and take account of the fact that he is a separate person, that his is the only life he has. *He* does not get some over-balancing good from his sacrifice, and no one is entitled to force this upon him – least of all a state or government that claims his allegiance (as other individuals do not) and that therefore scrupulously must be *neutral* between its citizens.
>
> (Nozick, 1974, pp. 32–3, author's emphasis)

For Nozick, it is illegitimate to use one person for the benefit of another. What makes this argument distinctive is the assertion that there is no such entity as the social good, just individual notions of what it is good to pursue and individually held property that may assist in achieving those ends.

This leads Nozick to state:

> There is no *central* distribution, no person or group entitled to control all the resources, jointly deciding how they are to be doled out. What each person gets, he gets from others who give to him in exchange for something, or as a gift. In a free society, diverse persons control different resources, and new holdings arise out of the voluntary exchanges and actions of persons . . . The total result is the product of many individual decisions which the different individuals are entitled to make.
>
> (Nozick, 1974, pp. 149–50)

From this starting point Nozick develops the idea of a just distribution based on entitlement to property or, as he terms it, *holdings*. This consists of three principles. The first principle derives from the *original acquisition of holdings*, or 'the appropriation of unheld things' (p. 150). Thus 'A person who acquires a holding in accordance with the principle of justice in acquisition is entitled to that holding' (p. 151). We are entitled to own something because we are the first ones to acquire it.

Second, which in practice would be the main form, there is the *transfer of holdings*, which deals with voluntary exchanges and gifts. Thus 'A person who acquires a holding in accordance with the principle of justice in transfer, from someone else entitled to the holding, is entitled to the holding' (p. 151). This is when we voluntarily exchange things with others in return for compensation or because we wish to gift it to others.

No one is entitled to a holding, according to Nozick, except by repeated applications of these two principles. However, some holdings have derived from fraud, enslavement or other illegitimate action. There is therefore the need for a third principle, which Nozick refers to as 'the rectification of injustice in holdings' (p. 152). This deals with the question: 'If past injustice has shaped present holdings in various ways, some identifiable, some not, what now, if anything, ought to be done to rectify these injustices?' (p. 152).

These three principles determine whether an individual's holdings are just and 'If each person's holdings are just, the total set (distribution) of holdings is just' (p. 153). In some ways Nozick is again demonstrating the typical libertarian position, which sees the matter of distribution as being determined by production (Barry, 1986). Thus, if we have legitimate ownership of property, the issue of its distribution is settled: we get what we are entitled to.

There are only two exceptions that Nozick will allow to these principles. First, our rights are constrained to the extent that we do not coerce others: we have exclusive use of our property, but not to the extent of placing our knife in the chest of another. Whilst we can portray Nozick's libertarianism as complete licence, the impact of his emphasis on what he terms *side constraints* would be a major limitation to individual action that would make any resulting society much more similar to current Western democracies than many of his critics (and perhaps Nozick himself) would admit. The other exception Nozick makes is the need for a night-watchman state to enforce contracts between individuals. But crucial to Nozick's theory is that such a state can arise without coercion. However, any further development of the state beyond the minimal level of protecting property rights and enforcing contracts would be coercive because of its redistributive nature.

According to Nozick, a key distinction between his theory of justice and others is that not only is his theory historical, but it also does not specify a particular pattern or end result. In this way, he connects up justice and individual freedom. A patterned principle is one that prescribes the form of distribution or prejudges outcomes within a society. Thus it is where a particular distribution (an end result) is seen as just. However, for Nozick, this situation *cannot* be just, as it involves the continual interference with individual liberty to maintain this pattern of distribution. It is here that Nozick uses his famous 'Walt Chamberlain' example. This is a thought experiment whereby he imagines a community in which income equality is established. Throughout a particular season many individuals choose to pay a voluntary premium to watch a particularly talented basketball player (Chamberlain), which is paid to the player. Chamberlain is so good that many are prepared to pay their additional voluntary sum. Accordingly, at the end of the year the basketball player is much wealthier than anyone else is in the community. But this has arisen entirely from voluntary acts, and entirely without coercion. Nozick questions the basis on which it would be acceptable to return to strict equality, a situation that could only be arrived at by considerable and continual intervention, when the inequality had derived entirely from voluntary acts.

We can summarise this brief discussion of Nozick's philosophy by saying that he believes maximising individual freedom is the supreme purpose of any society and this can only be attained through respecting property rights and limiting the role of the state. We might suggest that his position is an extreme – he advocates no state welfare provision but an almost complete reliance on private charity – but it does demonstrate what it would mean to have a society based on individual property rights in which all relations were within markets and not between individuals and the state.

Property and social relations

A somewhat different view is taken by conservative thinkers, who see property ownership as forming the basis of the type of society they wish to see. However, this is not just because of the role of markets, but also because of the fact that property rights create social relations: owning things, and the consequent need to transfer and exchange things, means we have to relate to others around us. We might suggest, therefore, that operating within markets is the way in which societies are created and develop. This is not, however, because they maximise individual freedom but rather because they create social obligations and so strengthen the bonds within society. Property ownership, for conservatives, has the virtue of giving individuals a stake in society and so an interest in its maintenance.

This view on property can be seen in the thought of Roger Scruton (2001) who discusses what he calls our 'absolute and ineradicable need for private property' (p. 92). He justifies this ineradicable need by stating that:

Ownership is the primary relation through which man and nature come together. It is therefore the first stage in the socialising of objects, and the condition of all higher institutions. It is not necessarily a product of greed or exploitation, but it is necessarily a part of the process whereby people free themselves from the power of things, transforming resistant nature into compliant image. Through property man imbues his world with will, and begins therein to discover himself as a social being.

(Scruton, 2001, p. 92)

As Scruton states, 'Through property an object ceases to be a mere inanimate thing, and becomes instead the focus of rights and obligations' (p. 93). Through property ownership 'the object is lifted out of mere "thinghood" and rendered up to humanity' (p. 93). It bears the imprint of social relations and reflects back to the owner 'a picture of himself as a social being' (p. 93), as someone now with the capability of relations with others. Property ownership is therefore seen by Scruton as a primary social relation. It is what allows us access to the social world, as beings able to achieve our ends.

This is a rather philosophical way of saying that without property we cannot identify any object in the world as our own, and hence we have no right to use any object, nor can we expect others to allow us access to it (not that they could, of course, because they too would have no rights over it). Without rights of ownership everything is merely an object of desire. Objects without ownership can play no part in social relations: there can be no exchange, no gifts and no transfers from one person to another.

Scruton argues that, if people are to become fully aware of themselves as agents who are capable of independent action within a social whole, then they need to see the world in terms of rights, responsibility and freedom. He suggests that it is 'The institution of property [that] allows them to do this' (p. 93). By making an object mine, I can now use it for my own purposes. I am able to be more active because my possibilities have been increased. But I have also been given a responsibility, for I now have to determine how it can be used, whether I should share my access, and so on.

Scruton therefore emphasises the social nature of property and markets by showing how it connects humans together and gives them responsibilities and the need to respect others: what is theirs is not mine, and what is mine is not theirs. If I want what is not mine then I must engage with others through negotiation, trade or persuasion rather than brute force. We might here return to the discussion on responsibility in chapter 2 and see a similarity with Schmidtz's argument about internalising responsibility. Indeed, Schmidtz argues that the main manner in which the internalisation of responsibility is to be achieved is precisely through the ownership of private property.

Having given this rather abstract justification of property ownership, Scruton then identifies the main form of property we experience. Ownership, as it were, grounds the self into the social world. As he states, instead of being at loose in the world, an individual is 'at home' (p. 93). He goes on:

> It is for this reason that a person's principal proprietary attitude is towards his immediate surroundings – house, room, furniture – towards those things with which he is, so to speak, mingled. It is the home, therefore, that is the principal sphere of property, and the principal locus of the gift.
>
> (Scruton, 2001, p. 93)

The most important form of property is the home, as this is the primary relationship with things in the world. It is what we live within and what therefore becomes part of us. When we own those things around us – the house and its contents – we are better able to control our surroundings and fulfil our personal and social obligations. The family unit is where we show responsibility to others, where our primary obligations are held and where we are most able to express our generosity.

We can see a ready connection here with policies pursued by Conservative (and other) politicians in the UK, who have encouraged property ownership through tax relief on mortgages, the Right to Buy and the subsidisation of equity sharing and shared ownership. Mrs Thatcher, in particular, argued that home ownership created a stake in society and gave households a common purpose. We might question the extent of this, as many academics and commentators have done, but it was undoubtedly an influential view and one that has persisted in UK housing policy ever since.

Property as capital

Property ownership is only meaningful if others recognise the fact. In countries like the USA and the UK, we can prove ownership of our house and that the car is ours. We have the deeds and registration documents. Moreover, there is a formal legal system that will back up our claims. If someone tries to take my car, I have a form of redress that either prevents them or allows me to claim compensation and demand punishment. We have a visible sign of our ownership and this is supported by what Hernando De Soto calls a 'representational process' (2000, p. 7).

However, as De Soto states, 'Third World and former communist nations do not have this representational process' (2000, p. 7). This means that they cannot use their capital, their resources, as they might wish. As De Soto states:

The single most important source of funds for new businesses in the United States is a mortgage on the entrepreneur's house. These assets can also provide a link to the owner's credit history, an accountable address for the creation of reliable and universal public utilities, and a foundation for the creation of securities.

(De Soto, 2000, p. 7)

In the USA, having a system that recognises property rights allows for the creation of businesses and therefore more wealth. This substantiates the point we made earlier, that property ownership needs a framework of law for markets to operate.

However, in the developing world this representational process does not exist. In sub-Saharan Africa that ready system of accountability is not there, with the result that proving ownership of land involves a lengthy and time-consuming process, perhaps involving bribing public officials in order to obtain permission (Boudreaux, 2008). De Soto shows that this is also a problem in Latin America, parts of post-communist Europe and other parts of Africa. The problem is that individuals and businesses have no straight-forward and dependable means of achieving recognition of their rights to property.

De Soto argues, therefore, that the problem for developing countries is not a lack of capital but its recognition. He states that even in poor countries like Haiti and Egypt the poor save: 'In Egypt, for instance, the wealth that the poor have accumulated is worth fifty-five times as much as the sum of all direct foreign investment ever recorded there, including the Suez Canal and the Aswan Dam' (2000, p. 6). The poor, however, hold their resources in what he calls 'defective forms', for example, 'houses built on land whose ownership rights are not adequately recorded' (p. 6).

So it is not the lack of possessions that is the problem, rather how they can, or in fact cannot, be used:

Because the rights to these possessions are not adequately documented, these assets cannot readily be turned into capital, cannot be traded outside of narrow local circles where people know and trust each other, cannot be used as collateral for a loan and cannot be used as a share against an investment.

(De Soto, 2000, p. 6)

But all these things are possible in the developed world. Accordingly, De Soto by default demonstrates what a formal structure of property ownership achieves in a market: it provides a title to things – we can prove they are ours; we can trust others and they can trust us because of the system that underpins our relations; and so we are able to use our property to improve our own situation and society as a whole.

In our consideration of property and prices we have looked at what makes markets work and, in doing so, made some tentative links to housing. However, we now need to be more explicit and look at housing markets. The first point I want to look at is just why it is that housing is more amenable to markets than other so-called welfare goods.

The nature of housing

As we have seen in chapter 2, Levine (1995) helps us to understand the nature of markets and how they differ from state action by looking at how they relate to wants and needs. Wants are things 'we choose for ourselves as a way of expressing who we are' (pp. 31–2). The most appropriate vehicle for exercising choice and self-expression is the market. A want is something desirable and we may consider it necessary, but it might be something we can live without, even if we might find it hard to actually do so.

The importance of this distinction is that it allows us to connect up the rather general discussion on markets that we have had so far with the nature of housing. In particular, we need to understand why housing is apparently so amenable to market provision.

Most European countries have compulsory state-funded education and some form of compulsory social insurance system to provide for health care and retirement. However, their provision of housing is by no means as comprehensive. Nowhere is this more marked than in the UK with its National Health Service, providing health care free at the point of access, but also with a large owner occupied sector provided by markets.

This suggests that there is something important that influences market activity in housing when compared with health and education. So why is it that a vast majority of housing is provided by markets but only a small minority of health care and education?

Of course, it might be entirely arbitrary or as a result of some historical accident. The post-war Attlee government (1945–51) nationalised health care and introduced National Insurance, but never got round to nationalising the housing stock and major housebuilders. Perhaps if they had stayed in office longer, or if the economic conditions had been different, then they might have done so. But this would still leave us with the question of why the Attlee government decided to tackle the structure of health care provision before housing. What was it about health care as compared with housing? After all, the war had seen 450,000 dwellings either destroyed or made uninhabitable with a further 3 million dwellings damaged to some extent (Malpass and Murie, 1999).

More recently we can point to the fact that expenditure on social housing has declined by over two-thirds since 1980, yet the Labour government elected in 1997 has more than doubled expenditure on health care (Wilcox, 2008). Yet still the issues that have been important in recent UK general elections and caused the most political controversy have not been homelessness or the allocation of social housing. Rather what is deemed to motivate voters is spending on health care and education.[2] So why is it that health and education are treated differently, and what has this to do with markets?

We can start to answer this by looking at the manner in which social provision is provided in the UK. Health and education are provided *universally*, in that they are available to all citizens regardless of income. They are provided on the basis of need rather than the ability to pay and so are available to the poorest and richest alike. However, social housing – and this has always been the case since its inception in the immediate post- World War I period – is provided as a *particularist* service. Social housing has always been susceptible to a means test that determines eligibility and it has never been the case that social provision is intended for all the population (King, 2003). Indeed until 1948 access to local authority housing in England was restricted to the 'working classes' only.

We might suggest that this is a matter of spending priorities and available resources: housing is an expensive commodity and so government naturally targeted its resources on those most in need. Yet this answer won't do, because health care is also expensive, but a government dealing with post-war reconstruction committed itself to free health care for all.

The reason for the differential treatment of housing and health is not really down to money or income but is essentially one of knowledge. In short, we can and do know more about our housing needs than our health care requirements. We can know that we are ill and in pain, but this does not mean that we know the cause of that pain nor the treatment necessary to alleviate it. We therefore have to rely on an expert to diagnose and treat the ailment. Moreover, we can seldom rely on past knowledge to assist us and, even if we could, we would still lack the expertise to treat the problem.

But there is a further problem. The need for health care is contingent on circumstance and so the need is often unpredictable, in that we do not know when or if we are to be ill. All of these issues create very difficult problems for comprehensive market provision. There may be a tendency for there to be underprovision in such systems, particularly amongst the poor, who may choose to spend their limited resources elsewhere (King and Oxley, 2000).

Table 3.3   The nature of housing

Housing need is:

- permanent;
- predictable;
- understandable.

But this is not the case with housing, even though it is an expensive commodity (see Table 3.3). First, our housing need is *permanent*, as we will always need housing, regardless of our circumstances (King, 1998). What differs, of course, is whether it is currently fulfilled or not. Second, because we always need housing, this means that it is *predictable*, allowing for a more regular pattern of provision. Of course, our need may change as we start a family and become more affluent, and then downsize as we get older, but this is not often due to any sudden change that demands an immediate intervention like an emergency operation. Barring war and natural disaster, there is therefore the ability to plan any change in a predictable manner. One other way of looking at this is to suggest that the stakes are often lower with housing than with health care. Poor quality housing may indeed be serious and need sorting out as quickly as possible, but poor health or a sudden illness clearly requires a more rapid response.

Third, as housing is both permanent and predictable, with a slower and more regular pattern of change, it is more readily *understandable*, in that we know we need it, that we will always need it and to what standard we require it (King, 1998, 2003). Even when we ask homeless people, they are entirely capable of telling us what constitutes good housing and they can recognise it when they see it. Unlike the case of health care, we do not require an expert to tell us that the housing is good and fits our needs.

These three principles – permanence, predictability and understandability – suggest that decision making in housing can be devolved more readily to the level of the household and thus housing is more amenable to choice. This does not mean we can build or maintain our dwelling ourselves (although we might), but that we have sufficient knowledge to set the parameters and determine what we need.

This returns us to the important issue of how much knowledge we need in order to operate in a market. As we have seen, the idea of perfect competition, which is the model that markets are judged by, is where consumers have perfect knowledge of the goods in a market, in terms of price and quality. As in the street market they are deemed capable of finding out all the necessary information on price and quality. But, as we have seen, both

Hayek (1982, 1988) and Sowell (2007) argue that the virtue of markets is precisely that we need *not* have this total knowledge. All we need be aware of is our own needs, and then what is available and whether we can afford it. This is provided by price, which operates as a signal, and that is all the knowledge we need in a market. Moreover, we only need to know this when we enter the market: if we are not looking to buy or rent a dwelling, we do not need to know anything about house prices or rents. Also we do not need to be aware of the intentions of others, such as landlords and developers, merely the price of the goods they are offering. According to Hayek, this makes markets much more efficient that any other planning mechanism. Hayek suggests that, if we summate the total knowledge of all consumers, it will far outweigh that of any planning body, and he argues that a market is precisely this summation.

So we can suggest that housing is more amenable to choice within markets. The nature of housing, being predictable, permanent and understandable, makes it compatible with individualised decision making in a way that is perhaps not possible with other complex welfare goods. However, this does not mean that housing markets operate perfectly. Indeed, they may work rather badly from time to time, especially if we take meeting everybody's housing need as the key measure. However, housing markets clearly do operate and can be said to work in that most people are well housed most of the time. But governments quite naturally need to concentrate on those who are not well housed and this means they need to intervene in housing markets. But to do so, they need to understand more about how housing markets work, and this is what we turn to next to complete this chapter.

The nature of housing markets

At the time of writing (May 2008) there was little good to say about housing markets. The collapse of the sub-prime housing market in the USA created serious repercussions in financial markets across the world. Many of the world's largest banks, like Credit Suisse and HSBC, announced huge losses on their investments and had to raise extra capital. Banks stopped lending to each other and this led to the collapse of the British bank, Northern Rock, in late 2007. The UK government stepped in to prop up Northern Rock and eventually had to take it into public ownership. Whilst all this was happening, mortgage lenders increased their interest rates on borrowing and withdrew some of their products. The Bank of England reduced interest rates yet this had no effect on the mortgage market, with lenders, who were finding it hard to obtain new funds, increasing their rates to borrowers.

Accordingly, UK house prices started to fall and an increasing sense of uncertainty and gloom about the housing market developed. Many of the big house builders reduced or even stopped new development and the levels of activity in the housing market declined by over 20 per cent compared to 2007.

So from this position we could quite properly argue that housing markets do not work terribly well: many households, particularly the young, could not afford to become owner occupiers and others were struggling to afford their mortgage repayments. The response of the UK Prime Minister, Gordon Brown, was to claim that things may not be good but were much worse elsewhere, which is not exactly a ringing endorsement of markets across the world.

So housing markets in 2008 were not in good shape and this might lead us to suggest that markets do not work well. We might suggest that markets were failing to operate in the manner we might have expected, and this being so, we might argue that markets should not be the main means by which housing needs are fulfilled. What it certainly does show is that markets in reality are much more complex than the model of perfect competition would suggest.

Indeed the idea of *market failure* is commonly used with regard to housing markets. This is an important concept, in that it forms the major justification for government intervention: markets fail and so government has to intervene to regulate current provision or to increase supply.

Market failure can be defined as 'where the conditions necessary for a market efficient allocation do not exist' (Oxley and Smith, 1996, p. 9). Market failure is therefore precisely when markets do not operate according to the simple model of perfect competition. It is when the market does not provide what is demanded at the cheapest possible price. This does not mean, of course, that markets do not work at all, but rather that they fail to be as efficient as economic theory states they could be. The problem of market failure is seen as being particularly prevalent in housing markets (Barlow

Table 3.4   Housing market failure

- Externalities.
- Longevity of the housing stock.
- Need for long-term finance.
- Equity and social and political issues.
- Inelasticity of supply.

---

and Duncan, 1994; Hills, 1991; Maclennan, 1982; Oxley and Smith, 1996). We therefore need to look at some of the reasons for this failure, which are summarised in Table 3.4.

Externalities

Markets create *externalities*, where the actions of consumers and producers have an impact, positively or negatively, on a third party or on society more generally. We might see this as a *social cost* or *social benefit* that is borne by society as a result of private decisions taken by individuals and businesses.

The classic example of an externality is industrial pollution caused by the production of goods and services. These goods are in demand and so suppliers are prepared to produce them. Yet the effect of industrial production is pollution, which places a cost on society as a whole. The cost of dealing with industrial pollution is a negative externality which has to be borne either by society, other individuals or businesses in other areas. In terms of housing, if we fail to maintain our property it can impact on our neighbours, have a negative effect on house values and quality of life, cause a nuisance to others, and so on.

However, the problem with dealing with externalities, be they positive or negative, is that they are often difficult to quantify as they frequently depend on the subjective perception of individuals (Shand, 1990). For example, my neighbour's attitude towards noise and nuisance may be very tolerant and so she is prepared to put up with my musical taste, whereas someone else might complain very quickly or even move away (King and Oxley, 2000). What this suggests is that we can point to external costs but perhaps find it hard to quantify them and so struggle to deal with them in any systematic manner.

Seldon (2004) states that it is entirely possible to deal with externalities through legal requirements to 'internalise' the external costs. This can be done by insisting that cars are fitted with anti-pollution devices, that hostels follow fire regulations, that environmental health laws are complied with, and so on. This is again to return to Schmidtz's point about the internalisation of responsibility, so that the costs of dealing with an externality are borne by the perpetrator. However, the issue for Seldon is whether the remedies are taken too far and impose an unreasonable and disproportionate cost, which affects those on low incomes. An example might be the imposition of regulations on landlords which increase their costs to the extent that they leave the market and so reduce the availability of housing for low income households. Crucially there is no exact method for determining the proportionality of costs in that landlords and their potential tenants have different thresholds regarding their preparedness to absorb additional costs.

Longevity

An issue allied to that of externalities is that individuals acting in their own self-interest do not necessarily think of future generations. However, housing is a long-lived asset, which is expensive to provide and to maintain (Hills, 1991). Once housing has been provided it is not easy to remedy its failings and it is wasteful to replace it. Most households live in 'second-hand' housing and many own dwellings that are older than they are. This means that the quality that we build housing to has an impact not just on us, but also on future generations. In general, the number of amenities in a dwelling increases over time and so the need for space increases. But it is very hard to predict what future needs will be. Therefore a household might only be concerned with their immediate needs and not consider those who are not yet born who will expect amenities not yet invented. Yet, if a dwelling has to survive and be viable for a century then some means have to be found to deal with the needs of future generations when we build today.

Borrowing

Housing is an expensive commodity that normally has to be financed by borrowing. It is very rare that we are able to pay cash for a dwelling, rather we need to take out a mortgage with arrangements to pay off the loan over say 25 or 30 years. But this introduces uncertainty with regard to our future income, fluctuations in repayments due to changes in interest rates, changes in house values and so on.

It is important to remember that when we buy a house we will not know exactly how much it has cost until we have made our last mortgage payment. Changes in interest rates will mean that our monthly costs might increase or decrease, and potentially the changes might be quite dramatic, as was indeed the case in the UK in the early 1990s when interest rates peaked at 15 per cent.

More recently the credit crunch and the problems following the crisis over Northern Rock in 2007 and its nationalisation in 2008 indicate how decisions made several years ago can be transformed by unforeseen circumstances. The policies of Northern Rock, in aggressively trying to increase its market share in the mortgage market, made the bank financially unviable when global credit conditions changed in mid-2007. Importantly, this did not just affect the housing market but also the availability of credit more generally. Likewise, households who took out a large mortgage when interest rates were low might find themselves struggling to maintain their repayments if interest rates increase. So we can see that the need to borrow to fund house purchases can create uncertainty in the housing market and in the wider economy.

Equity

Even such a keen exponent of markets as Hayek (1988) admits that they are not fair, in that they do not distribute resources according to merit or the amount of effort exerted or, indeed, according to need. Markets are impersonal entities to the extent that they guarantee no one anything just because they might need it. Hayek's support for markets is entirely based on the utilitarian argument that they lead to far better outcomes than any other form of social organisation. Markets are not perfect; just the least worst option.

Yet it might be that a society places fairness or social justice above economic efficiency or the entitlement to property. This society might find it unacceptable that some people, who were 'born lucky', have more than enough, whilst others, who have worked hard all their lives, end up with very little. Some people inherit considerable housing wealth from their parents and this can be seen simply as a matter of luck. The inheritors have done nothing to deserve this wealth (other than being related). A society might therefore seek to moderate these effects by intervening in a market.

This problem is exacerbated by the relatively high cost of housing, which means that there is a trade-off between quality and affordability, which raises issues of the distribution of resources (King and Oxley, 2000). If some people are left poor as a result of the operation of a market, then a government might wish to control that market so it works more for the benefit of the poor. Government, of course, might not succeed in its efforts, but this does show that there are other priorities than market efficiency. This had led some commentators, such as Wolff (1991), to criticise Nozick's principles concerning the entitlement to holdings. Wolff argues that these principles might be rigorous, but is it fair and reasonable that some people are left destitute while others are rich? Therefore we might see social justice, equity or poor relief as more important than the inviolability of individual rights to property.

Inelasticity

The supply of housing in the short run is *inelastic* (Barlow and Duncan, 1994). This means that supply does not respond proportionately or immediately to changes in demand. Therefore, if demand for housing in an area increases, it does not follow that there is an immediate increase in supply. Indeed, increases in supply can take a number of years to come through. The result of this inelasticity of supply is an increase in price. There are a number of reasons why this inelasticity occurs.

First, there are limits to how far we can increase the productivity of housing. The construction industry tends to be labour intensive with the need for specialist trades such as bricklayers, plasterers and electricians. On top of this, the fallout from the failure of high-rise development in the UK, USA and Europe in the 1950s and 1960s led to a justifiably cautious approach towards experimental design (Power, 1993). Planners and developers are rightly cautious of untried techniques and tend to trust what is known and, importantly, what is popular. Most households like traditional housing designs, such as low-rise housing located within green space. This might, however, make development more expensive, particularly the cost of land, and so extend the period in which housing supply catches up with demand.

Second, there is one crucial way in which housing differs from most other goods and services. Housing lacks mobility, in that it cannot be moved from one place to another in response to changes in demand. If there is a shortage of apples in Peterborough, a new supply can be transported in by plane and truck relatively quickly. However, a shortage of housing can only be alleviated by building more housing in that area. The alternative is to encourage or persuade some households to move to other areas where housing is in plentiful supply. This is an important aspect of housing markets and accounts for many of the policy interventions in England since 2000, which has seen the establishment of growth areas in the south, where large amounts of new housing is planned, alongside the demolition of supposedly unwanted housing in the Midlands and the north. Interestingly, the latter policy is referred to as *housing market renewal*, with the idea that the market is renewed by government intervention to replace outdated and unwanted housing with a smaller amount of new affordable housing (ODPM, 2003). What this example apparently demonstrates is that there are markets in one part of a country that need intervention because of a shortage of affordable housing, whilst at the same time there are other markets where there is insufficient demand for the amount of housing available, a problem that can also apparently be remedied by government intervention.

Third, there are what Maclennan (1982) has referred to as *spatial and situational restrictions* on the supply of housing. This includes planning restrictions on development that seek to protect other households. Households can only extend their dwelling or developers only build a new estate if it is reasonable and does not impinge on others. A relevant issue is that land is scarce, particularly in urban areas, and so there might be competing uses. Large companies, such as supermarket chains, want to be located near housing and transport systems but local residents might object to this development. Other residents might treasure the green space that surrounds their housing and therefore complain at proposals to develop on this space, even though there is unmet demand for housing. Clearly, land availability is an important restriction on housing development. Government might seek to deal with this by encouraging building on brownfield sites by offering subsidies or setting targets.

Some parts of the UK will be seen as more desirable locations than others, with the result that housing is more expensive in these areas. In some locations there might be a relatively high proportion of the housing that is used for holiday lets or second homes. These dwellings might be unused for much of the year, as well as having the effect of increasing overall house prices in the area. This is particularly a problem in rural areas, where average wages are low, or in seaside areas where employment is seasonal. The effect of second homes might therefore be to price local people out of the housing market. Indeed, the market signals offered are precisely for more holiday accommodation rather than housing for low-income households.

All these factors can limit the supply of new housing or cause delays in increasing supply. As a result, government might feel it needs to intervene to speed up the process, either by directly subsidising provision or by easing planning restrictions. However, some supporters of markets, such as Seldon (2004), argue that whilst markets have faults, these can also be readily remedied. Markets, Seldon states, are corrigible – they are capable of correction – whilst the faults of the state are not. This leads us in the direction of the role of the state, to which we now turn.

Think point

Why is buying and selling housing so complex? Does it have to be so?

Conclusions

This chapter, like the previous one, has been largely conceptual and has only lately turned to consider housing directly. What we have been concerned with is what markets are and how they work. We have stressed both the importance of prices and property to markets in something of an abstract manner.

Yet, as we have seen in the last section, there is a purpose here. Much of the housing in modern developed countries is provided in markets, and so we need to understand why this is possible and what it involves. There is also the fact that the main justification for government intervention is that markets do not work properly. Much of the rest of this book focuses on the role of the state and how this interacts with markets. In essence we can see housing finance as the means by which housing markets work and how they are regulated and adjusted by government action. Hence this general discussion on markets has set up the discussion on what the state actually does and what housing finance is used for.

Finally, despite the apparent existence of market failure, markets do exist and they clearly do work. The role of housing markets has expanded over the last 25 years to the extent that 80 per cent of UK households have found their housing through them, a situation that is similar in many European countries, as well as the USA. Therefore, we should not overstate problems and give the impression that they are fatal. What it rather suggests is that we should be sceptical of ideals and not see the key question as being markets *or* government, but how much of each we see as desirable and effective.

Further reading

The literature on markets is absolutely huge, but those seeking an introduction should seek out Thomas Sowell's *Basic Economics* (3rd edition, 2007), which gives a comprehensive coverage of economic theory with some useful examples and with not one single graph or equation to be seen – and is all the better for it. The most useful book on housing economics is Michael Oxley's *Economics, Planning and Housing* (2004), which provides a full discussion of relevant policy debates in the UK, Europe and the USA. For those wanting a debate on the role of markets and the state, covering issues like externalities and the role of economic policy, see *Housing: Who Decides?* (2000) by myself and Michael Oxley.

4

Government action

Learning outcomes

- What government is and what it does.
- The nature of housing subsidies.
- What social housing is for.
- The effects of government intervention.

Introduction

We ended our discussion on markets with a section on how they might fail and then government might need to intervene in order to deal with this failure. So government might need to regulate and apportion costs as a result of externalities, or it might need to intervene with subsidies to speed up the production of dwellings. So we might say that government action is necessary because of market failure. But this is to see the role of government as being entirely reactive, and only having a role when, and if, markets fail.

Can we not point to a more positive role for government? Certainly it is clear that markets can only operate within a framework of legal protection and enforcement, and this implies some form of agency that is external to a market with sufficient status to oversee its operation. But this still implies a rather minimalist role, perhaps akin to that advocated by Nozick (1974) in his idea of the night-watchman state, existing only for the protection of property rights and defence against threats.

But government does much more than this, and most people do not object to it in the manner that Nozick did. Indeed, we can suggest that most governments intervene much more than merely to correct market failure.

Governments in developed economies provide free schooling, and in fact make it compulsory for children to be educated up to a certain age. They might also provide free or subsidised health care that goes beyond dealing with emergencies. Most governments are concerned with what they term 'public health', which involves a concern for issues like obesity, alcohol and drug consumption and sexual health. Government, therefore, is very active and is seen as having a positive role.

In chapter 2 we offered what might be seen as a justification of this positive role, namely, the concept of need and the supposition that needs are best met by government action rather than markets. We saw need as something defined externally from the individual or group concerned. This was because needs do not have to be things of which we are conscious; we might be blissfully unaware. So we might carry on eating or drinking to excess unaware of the damage we are doing to our bodies until one day we collapse due to alcohol poisoning or a heart attack. We would then require immediate care and attention. But on what basis could we be sure that the care and attention is there, and wouldn't it be better for us to have received a warning before we had damaged ourselves irreparably?

Of course, we might say that we have the choice to eat and drink ourselves to death, but to return again to the discussion in chapter 2, is this responsible? What if we are in a coma and not dead, so that some agency or individual now has to look after us? Is it fair that our family should take on this responsibility, and that they do it, even if they disapproved of our drinking? And what if they simply could not afford to look after us? Should we be left to die? Most of us would not feel comfortable with this idea of being neglected when we are incapable of doing anything for ourselves, and I would also suggest that most of us would appreciate knowing that something is dangerous so that at least we can consider moderating our behaviour accordingly. And if we do not know always what is right for us to do, then who or what does?

So if we have needs, we must also be concerned with who can best recognise these needs. If we lack the capability to do it, then it must fall on somebody or something else. The presumption in a modern society is that this role can best be taken up by government.

Indeed, government in modern societies is ubiquitous. There is seldom an issue with which government is neither concerned nor urged to consider. Apparently the one thing a politician cannot do is *nothing*. It is not acceptable to say that the problem belongs to someone else or it is just bad luck, unfortunate or just one of those things. What this suggests is that government gets involved in a lot more than the meeting of immediate need. Of course, there are many issues that need government intervention, such as natural disasters and war, but this is not the same as planning for the provision of executive homes within commuter distance of London. On the basis of the discussion in chapter 3, we might have thought that this was best left to markets to provide.

But in a sense it is, because government does not actually build or pay for the executive homes. Rather, government decides where, when, and how many of them are to be provided in each area. It seeks to control and ration the provision of housing and so moderates the market behaviour of developers and households.

In other situations government does actually ensure an increase in development through direct provision and funding, and again this is justified on the basis of meeting need, albeit of a different sort: the homeless and vulnerable rather than commuter families. So intervention can be within markets and outside them: government can encourage activity and undertake it itself.

In this chapter we shall explore why government intervenes and provides finance for housing. First, we explore what government is and how it differs from the state. We need to do this because of the idea that government has an interest and that this may differ from other parts of society. In particular, there may be disparities between local state agencies and central government. This is important in housing as all housing, by definition, is local, but much of the funding, due to the high capital cost, comes from the centre.

Second, we shall explore what government does that cannot be done elsewhere; what things only government can do, and which would not be done if there were no government. Inevitably this will be speculative in that government, of one sort or another, has always existed. This will lead into the third part of the chapter, which looks in some detail at the manner in which government actually can and does subsidise housing. We explore what subsidies are, what types might be used and what effect they have. This leads then into a discussion on the direct provision of housing – social housing – and its purpose.

Lastly, in this chapter we shall consider what might be called government failure – the idea that government might not be that successful in providing goods and services and that this should best be left to markets. This problem of government failure might arise because government is inefficient, or because, as we said in chapter 3, individuals are more capable of determining and meeting their housing needs than other important welfare goods like health and education. The focus here, however, is on the inevitability of unintended consequences.

This discussion will be rather brief, particularly the sections on the role of government. This is not because we wish to ignore the full complexity of the issues, but rather because we wish to arrive at them as soon as possible. The discussions that follow this chapter are essentially concerned with what government actually does in practice, in terms of how it influences markets (chapter 5) and how it controls housing organisations, policies and practices through financial instruments (chapter 6). The rest of this book is therefore concerned with government action, and so what we need to do is merely introduce it and set up the discussion.

What is government?

We have suggested that government is ubiquitous; that it is everywhere and involved in many, if not all, activities. Yet we need to be clear what government is not, what its limits are and thus differentiate it from other concepts. So, for example, when we say that markets need to be underpinned by a legal framework, this is not necessarily provided by government but by the legal system and the courts, which enforce contracts and recognise and protect rights to property. Indeed, both government and the legal system are part of something larger, namely, the *state*.

But it is a common fault to equate the state with the government, and to see them as one and the same. We talk of state provision of housing and believe that this is provided by government; we talk of state funding and government funding as if they are interchangeable terms. So we need to be clear about our terms. This is not just to be pedantic or make academic distinctions, but rather it is of particular importance in housing, which is often provided by the state but locally in the form of municipal or local government. This provision may be assisted with government funding and regulation, and enabled by legislative backing (the legislature or parliament being another part of the state and separate itself from the government) but it is not the same as government provision.

So government is not the state. But what, then, is it? It is easier to answer this question by looking at what the state is and thus seeing what part government has within it.

MacCormack (1993) sees the state as 'a territorially organised political community, within which power is exercised over the territory with respect to economic resources available in it, and to the use of force in interpersonal relations' (pp. 125–6). He goes on to state that 'It is the normal claim of states that they have a monopoly over legitimate use of force in or in respect of the state territory' (p. 126). The state therefore exercises authority over a territory and over those who reside within it. Furthermore, this authority means the state has right of compulsion over its citizens and those who reside within its territory. We might summarise MacCormack's discussion with the definition of the state as *a compulsory political association that successfully claims the monopoly of physical force within a given territory*.

Only the state can legitimately use force to impose its authority on citizens or empower others on its behalf. So the state has the power to make political decisions and ensure that they are implemented, if necessary by force.

The state can be conceived of as an acting subject, in that it is considered to be a body in itself that acts, and so we might say that the British state does this or that. However, the state really acts through a series of individuals and organisations acting as the organs or representatives of the state. Obviously, the particular individuals and agencies differ according to the constitutional arrangements in any one country. But each country will have a head of state in the form of a monarch or president. In the USA the head of state is the president, whilst in the UK it is the Queen.

The head of state is also the head of the government, and so in the UK we refer to Her Majesty's Government. Of course, in practice the actual authority is no longer vested in the Queen but in her prime minister. The prime minister actually takes the executive decisions, but it is still formally done on behalf of Her Majesty.

The government is the body that undertakes the executive role of governing within a territory (its role is summarised in Table 4.1). This means it manages the affairs of the country and acts as the formal representative of the state to foreign powers. The government can set the agenda for a country and seek to lead it, often in a manner determined by elections. But the government is not the only agency within a state with power and authority.

In particular, we need to differentiate between the executive, which is Her Majesty's Government or the US or French presidents, and the legislature. This latter body is where laws are enacted and where finance is raised to undertake executive action. In most countries taxation can only be raised by the legislature, which also has the monopoly over statute law. In the USA the legislature is made up of the two houses of Congress (House of Representatives and the Senate), and in the UK, the two houses of Parliament

Table 4.1   What is government?

- Manages the affairs of the state.
- Implements a political programme.
- Leads the country and sets the political and economic agenda.
- Represents the state to foreign powers.
- Controls the armed forces.
- Influences the legislature.
- Dispenses (but does not raise) funds.

(Commons and Lords). In some countries, such as the USA, there is a complete separation between executive and legislature, with defined constitutional powers and different electoral arrangements. In other countries, like the UK, there is less formal separation, with the government being formed from the party that can claim a majority of support in the House of Commons. This has important consequences, in that it is much easier for a British prime minister to get his or her way with the legislature than a US president, who is not a member of the legislature and has less direct patronage and power over it.

The state also consists of other bodies that, as well as the executive and legislature, typically include the civil service or bureaucracy that run government departments, regional and local government, the armed forces, police and law courts. In some countries, for example in the USA, Germany and Australia, the state has a federal structure and has separate governments and legislatures at the regional level (confusingly often referred to as states!) which might also have some tax raising powers. In these countries formal constitutions record which powers are located where. However, this does not mean that there is no possibility of conflict. The United Kingdom has historically been the very opposite, with all power located within Parliament (and hence who controls it) and with no written constitution. Since 2000, however, there has been some devolution of power to an Assembly in Wales and Parliament in Scotland. But there is still no written constitution that definitely lays down what each part of the state may or may not do.

So we can see the government as the executive arm of the state. But, whilst this will hold in most situations, we need to complicate the picture a little on the basis of the discussion above. This is necessary because housing is rather different from other goods and services that government might provide. As we have stated, housing is provided locally, in that it must be physically located within specific communities. This is fundamentally different from the provision of national defence, which will be organised centrally and may be involved in activities thousands of miles away.

When we talk about government we therefore mean a number of things. First, it includes the executive, as we have discussed. The executive will be organised into a number of government departments looking after such issues as finance, foreign affairs, health, education, transport and, amongst many other things, housing. These departments will often be headed by a senior politician who will be part of the Cabinet where formal executive decisions are often taken. Each of these departments will consist of staff, known as civil servants, with the role of implementing executive decisions.

However, many decisions of government are taken by semi-autonomous bodies. In England, for example, a new body called the Homes and Communities Agency provides funding and regulation of housing associations.

The purpose of these bodies is to separate out policy making and operational activity, giving government ministers the ability to detach themselves from day-to-day responsibility, but without losing any control over policy or finance. They have tended to be used in cases in which government is supporting and funding non-statutory bodies. So, in the case mentioned above, housing associations are private companies and charities that are not formally accountable to government. Hence they are funded at arm's length to maintain that autonomy.

As we have stated above, many countries have regional or local governments that preside over particular areas. These bodies will have more limited powers, but they are important in that they are often involved in the direct provision of services, such as local policing, schools, transport and housing. Indeed, in the UK, a majority of social housing is still owned by local authorities. However, local authorities in the UK are of declining influence and are heavily circumscribed, with most of their funding coming from central government. This is not, though, the case in other countries, where regional government has a constitutional status including tax raising powers.

The existence of local and regional government is a major complicating factor in understanding government action, and this is of special importance to any discussion on housing. Central governments may plan, legislate and provide finance, but the actual policy is implemented by others, be they other layers of government (local authorities) or private bodies (housing associations). This is important because the interests of central and local government might differ because of particular local interests or different political control. An example was the dispute over housebuilding targets in the south of England in 2003 when a Labour central government insisted on certain numbers of new dwellings in high demand areas, many of which were under Conservative control. Many of these housing targets were seen by local politicians and the communities they represented as being too high. The matter was settled by adjudication through the courts, which found in favour of central government. But the result was a delay in meeting the government's targets, a lot of local resentment and eventually legislation produced by government to reduce the level of local intervention in the planning system. What this shows is that there is not necessarily a common interest between levels of government or between central government and local communities. The national interest, in this case of increasing the housing stock, was seen to conflict with local interests, such as maintaining the countryside and preserving quality of life. There is often no straightforward means of negotiating in these disputes except through the exercise of power, and what matters here are the specific constitutional and political arrangements that pertain.

What can government do?

So government is the executive part of the state which seeks to lead and direct the activities of that state. This implies that it is the most powerful element within a state, and this may indeed be the case. However, as we have seen above, this does not mean that its role is not challenged, or indeed that government always gets its way.

As we have suggested, the actual role taken by government will differ according to the particular state. This means that we cannot be too specific here in detailing what government is concerned with: the UK government is more powerful within its state than the US president or the Swiss federal government. However, we can point to four general functions undertaken by government (see Table 4.2). First, central government can *plan* and set the policy agenda. This might be through policy documents, commissioning and undertaking research, but also through the broad sweep of government fiscal and monetary policy. Second, the government can use its relationship with, or control over, the legislature. Most governments will have a *legislative programme*, which they seek to push through the legislature. In some countries, such as the UK, this is reasonably straightforward, assuming the government has a sufficient majority, but in some others that have separation of powers, such as the USA, this might be more difficult, especially when a president is coming towards the end of his second term and so cannot seek re-election. Third, government can attempt to *regulate* other bodies on the basis of its policies to ensure that they are implemented and its commitments fulfilled. Finally, and perhaps most important for us, is providing and directing *finance* towards particular policy objectives.

We can generalise that there are four stages starting with planning, moving to legislating, then regulating and financing. However, it would be rather too simplistic to suggest that these are all straightforward processes and that one follows on from the other. In particular, there is some overlap and interaction between the various functions. The provision of finance is often

Table 4.2   What government does

Government carries out four basic functions:

- planning action;
- legislating (or seeking to);
- regulating;
- funding.

Table 4.3 Actions only government can do

- Control and direct the economy.
- Take advantage of economies of scale and bulk purchasing.
- Override markets through fiscal and monetary policy and legislation.
- Take a strategic overview of the needs of the country and balance competing objectives.
- Try to achieve universality of provision.
- Try to attain uniformity of provision.
- Target provision on under-represented groups and areas of under-provision.

---

dependent on regulation, and new legislation might be proposed because of the failure of regulation.

Using these four functions we can point to a number of general actions that government can undertake that would be difficult for any other body, be it a market or an individual, to achieve. These actions might not apply to all states and, even where they do, we might not consider them all to be essential or necessary. Instead these are actions that are quite commonly undertaken by government (see Table 4.3).

First, government can attempt to control and direct the economy by persuading the legislature to raise taxes (often a formality in unitary states like the UK) and through its ability to set interest rates and its own spending. Government spending in developed countries tends to be between 30 to 50 per cent of gross domestic product, and so changes in this spending can have a considerable impact on the economy as a whole.

Second, we can suggest that central provision might lead to economies of scale, in that large, nationally organised bodies can have considerable market power. In most countries the armed forces are the main, if not sole, purchaser of defence equipment, and so they can seek to drive down costs on the basis that suppliers might find it hard to sell their goods elsewhere. Likewise, the National Health Service (NHS) in the UK, which provides 90 per cent of health care, is by far the largest purchaser of drugs in the country and so it has a considerable influence on drug prices in the UK. A decision not to allow the use of a drug in the NHS means that there is virtually no market for it. When this is allied to the government's role in regulating drugs, we can see that they can have a considerable effect on the prices drug companies can charge, with the hope that this makes provision cheaper than would otherwise be the case. The downside, of course, is that the NHS is effectively the market for drugs in the UK and so there is little in the way of competition to drive down prices: the issue therefore is whether government is capable of setting price levels properly.

This takes us to the third particular power of government. As government can raise taxes and make laws, it can override markets to allow for certain political targets to be met. It might be that society believes that issues such as social justice or equity outweigh a market efficient outcome. Ensuring all members of society are well housed might be seen as more important than consumer choice or free competition (King and Oxley, 2000). Related to this is the ability that government has to take a national overview of spending and market activity, and so attempt to balance competing objectives. Hence it is able to balance society's priorities for housing against those for health, transport, as well as for low taxes. Of course, a government may not achieve this, and indeed the particular sense of priorities might be contested: young drivers might place transport as a higher priority than the elderly, who might want more money spent on health care.

Fifth, governments might seek to attain universality in provision. It might be that certain goods and services are seen as so fundamental that they should be provided to all relevant persons at the point of need. Again the NHS is an example of this, but we can also point to old-age pensions, income maintenance and housing allowances as examples. Likewise, government can attempt to achieve some form of uniformity of provision across the country. We might feel that certain forms of provision should be available to all equally; for example, it is much more expensive to send a letter from London to the north of Scotland than, say, from one part of London to another, yet the Royal Mail charges the same for both on the basis of fairness. Likewise, paying a claimant's rent through a housing allowance system allows people to live in high rent areas.

Lastly, government can try to ensure that provision is at the right level and thus deal with market under-provision (King and Oxley, 2000). In particular, a market might not provide housing for some minority groups or for people with disabilities whose needs increase the cost of housing considerably (providing wheelchair access, grab rails, accessible showers, etc.).

So there are a number of things that government can claim to do that would be difficult for any other body to achieve. In particular, it can be

Think point

Which of the points in Table 4.3 do you think is the strongest justification for government action? Why?

argued that a market will fail to do some or all of these activities. The point of dispute, of course, is whether all of these are necessary and are worth the other elements that come with a powerful central government. These are issues that we shall return to later in the book, but now we shall look at how government subsidises housing.

Housing subsidies

We saw in chapter 3 that housing markets have certain peculiarities, which may mean that they do not work as efficiently as society would like. As a result, it is argued, government needs to intervene to correct these ineffici- encies and ensure that housing markets operate better. This may involve the direct provision of housing.

Thus one of the main ways in which the state intervenes in housing markets is by providing subsidies to landlords and households. This might be to make housing more affordable, to encourage landlords to build more or better quality housing, or to ensure the housing stock is of a sufficiently high quality. We therefore need to understand what role subsidies play. This will allow us a fuller understanding of the role of the state.

As a starting point we will try to define exactly what subsidies are. In simple terms, *subsidies are intended to make housing cheaper and more affordable than it otherwise would be*. Subsidies, therefore, are about altering the cost of housing and so potentially allowing more households access to it.

A rather more detailed definition is offered by Oxley and Smith (1996), who see a housing subsidy as 'An explicit or implicit flow of funds initiated by government activity which reduces the relative cost of housing production or consumption below what it otherwise would have been' (pp. 40–1).

This is a useful definition for a number of reasons. First, it is neutral, showing that subsidies can be used for all housing tenures. Whilst there is a tendency to concentrate on social housing, we need to be aware that governments also subsidise the private sector, through housing allowances and improvement grants, and owner occupiers through a variety of forms of tax relief and exemptions. Second, this definition does not just refer to the use of public funds. The reference to an implicit flow of funds can be seen as a reference to measures such as rent control, where private landlords effectively subsidise their tenants because they are not permitted to increase their rents above a ceiling set by government (see chapter 5 for a fuller discus- sion). The definition covers subsidies ranging from tax relief for owner occupiers to government grants to housing associations. Finally, it demon- strates that subsidies can be directed towards landlords to assist them in building, managing and maintaining dwellings, but also to the consumers

of housing in the form of tax relief or housing allowances. Subsidies can be used to support both production (supply) and consumption (demand).

Accordingly, any definition of a subsidy is also very much tied up with how it is used. For instance, subsidies paid to housing organisations, which allow them to build new dwellings at subsidised rents and to maintain their existing stock, have a markedly different purpose *and effect* on housing systems than subsidies paid to individuals to assist them in affording market rents. Subsidies to housing organisations assume we need more housing and are therefore explicitly aimed at increasing the supply. Subsidies paid to individuals will not necessarily encourage an increase in the supply of housing, but are rather intended to help households afford what already exists.

So subsidies aim to make housing more affordable. However, within this larger aim government might seek to achieve other objectives. We therefore need to look at the purpose of subsidies in more detail, and some examples from the UK will demonstrate this. When housing subsidies were introduced soon after World War I in the UK, their purpose was to deal with a shortage of good quality housing that all households could afford. Therefore the main purpose of subsidies was to deal with this shortage by encouraging local councils (and, later, housing associations) to build new housing and to regenerate existing dwellings to bring them up to modern standards of amenity.

But subsidies have been used to encourage particular forms of activity. For example, in the 1950s government encouraged slum clearance in England, but then in the 1970s the policy changed to one of rehabilitation of poor quality housing rather than knocking it down. Accordingly, the type of subsidy offered was tailored to meet these changed policy objectives. Another important example of how subsidies can direct action followed the *Housing Subsidies Act 1956*. This Act gave £22 annually per dwelling to local authorities to build traditional houses, but £66 annually per dwelling for flats of 15 storeys and above (Power, 1987). The effect was to encourage high-rise development even though these were more expensive to build and maintain and proved to be less popular than traditional housing. Power (1993) shows that similar policies were used in the USA and Europe to meet shortage, but from the 1970s onwards there was also a shift towards keeping communities together through regeneration and rehabilitation of the existing housing stock.

Yet subsidies also have a further, less open purpose, namely to control the activity of housing organisations. Subsidies can be used as financial leverage to force housing organisations to operate in a manner amenable to central government's aims. We can see here that the purpose of subsidies has moved away from the relatively straightforward notion of *subsidy-as-*

support to that of *subsidy-as-control*. Many policies introduced in Britain since the 1970s have been aimed at ensuring that local authorities fulfil the wider aims of government. Thus an important, but implicit, aim of housing subsidy is now to control activity rather than to encourage it.

This leads onto the second issue with regard to the purpose of subsidies, which relates to how and to whom they are distributed. First, there are subsidies that take the form of bricks and mortar or *object* subsidies. These are aimed at allowing landlords to provide new additional housing at subsidised rents. Between the end of World War I and the 1970s these subsidies dominated housing finance, being seen as the best way to deal with housing shortages; financial incentives were offered to encourage landlords to build dwellings. The main effect of these subsidies therefore was to increase the *supply* of housing, and thus they are therefore sometimes referred to as supply side subsidies, or capital subsidies.

Second, housing subsidies can take the form of tax relief to owner occupiers and housing allowances. These are referred to as *subject* or *personal* subsidies. The aim of these subsidies is to make housing more affordable by increasing household income. They therefore have the effect of increasing the *demand* for housing and are accordingly referred to as demand side subsidies. The purpose of subsidies is summarised in Table 4.4.

Since the 1970s there has been a shift in most developed countries away from object subsidies and towards subject subsidies. In the UK, for example, object subsidies accounted for over two-thirds of housing expenditure in 1976, but were down to less than a third by 2006.

Kemp (1997) has suggested three reasons for this general shift away from object subsidies. First, he cites the end of massive housing shortages in the 1970s as a result of the mass building programmes undertaken in Europe and elsewhere since 1945. This meant that a reassessment of what constituted the key housing problems was needed. Instead of the problem of shortage government's attention now turned to the shortage of income of some households as the key issue. Hence there began a shift towards income maintenance and the use of housing allowances as a means of ensuring low income households gain access to housing. If the problem was not one of shortage – if there was now enough housing – the issue was of access and affordability.

Table 4.4   The purpose of subsidies

- To encourage supply of housing (object subsidies).
- To increase the demand for the existing stock (subject subsidies).
- To influence activity in a particular direction.
- To control the activities of individuals and organisations.

Second, Kemp pointed to the general economic malaise of the 1970s, with high levels of unemployment coupled with high inflation in many countries. The result was a belief that the welfare state was unaffordable in its current form. Already certain demographic trends were becoming evident, particularly longer lifespans, and therefore it was felt that the welfare state was becoming an increasing burden at a time when governments were struggling to understand changes in the world economy. As housing, along with road building, is a very capital intensive activity, it was an easy target for cutbacks.

Third, Kemp points to a change in the political climate, as well as in the economy. He suggests there developed a general belief in market solutions to problems in social and public policy, emphasising the importance of the consumer over that of the producer of services. This was manifested by the election of right-wing governments in the USA, Germany and the UK, which survived for all of the 1980s and into the 1990s. This shift in political opinion was driven in part by the failing economy and the belief that the interventionist economic policies of the post-1945 era were no longer valid. But there was also an undoubted intellectual shift in favour of markets and smaller government.

This change in the balance between object and subject subsidies implies a change in the purpose of housing subsidies. Instead of subsidy being used to increase supply it is now aimed at bolstering demand. The belief is that there is enough housing for the number of households in the country. What is therefore at issue is not the *quantity* of housing, but whether all households can gain access to housing of sufficient *quality*.

But the two different forms of subsidy are based on two different sets of assumptions about the role of government and the competence of individual households: to favour demand side subsidies is to suggest the problem is one of a lack of income and that individuals are basically capable of choosing if given the resources; supply side subsidies carry the implication of a more fundamental problem that cannot be solved by increasing household income alone.

It is therefore worthwhile exploring some of these assumptions by looking at the two types of subsidies in more detail. It is fair to say that most academics and commentators believe that object subsidies are more effective in delivering housing for those on low incomes. These subsidies allow housing to be built and offered at sub-market rents, whilst also ensuring the housing is of high quality and is provided in high cost areas. Yet, as Kemp (1997) demonstrates, it is also true to state that these commentators have lost the argument, with governments since the 1970s favouring subject subsidies and with some governments like those in Australia, New Zealand and the Netherlands ending object subsidies altogether. However, object subsidies have not been abandoned entirely and so we can still gain by looking at why they were deemed to be justified. If for no other reason, a look at this form of subsidy will point up some of the purported problems with subject subsidies. Hence in the two sections that follow we can show that the justification for one form of subsidy also provides objections to the other.

The purpose of object subsidies

Throughout much of the twentieth century and in most developed countries the main form of housing support were object subsidies. We can suggest that this was largely aimed at dealing with housing shortages, but there are also a number of general arguments put forward by economists and others seeking to justify this form of subsidy.

Housing is a merit good

One of the most common such arguments is that housing is a merit good and it is therefore socially desirable to provide good quality housing. Merit goods can be defined as 'goods which society believes individuals should have but which some individuals decide not to purchase' (Oxley and Smith, 1996, p. 11). Oxley and Smith go on to relate this to housing provision by suggesting that 'Good quality housing can be viewed as a merit good which will bring benefits to individuals over and above those which individuals perceive' (p. 11) and that 'There is a case for governments encouraging the provision of merit goods which will inevitably be under-provided in a market system' (p. 11).

Merit goods are therefore goods that individuals ought to consume at a certain level, because it is good for them. However, they may not be fully aware of their benefits or may choose not to consume to the desired level. Thus there might be a discrepancy between what individuals wish to do and what society as a whole thinks is best. Therefore, according to this argument, there might still be a problem even if individuals received money themselves with which to purchase or rent houses – they may not use the money to purchase sufficiently 'good quality' housing.

However, we have already questioned this assumption in chapter 3 when we looked at the nature of housing. We argued that housing was more amenable to choice because the need for it was permanent, predictable and therefore understandable. Thus it might be the case that, for most, the issue is really one of income and not a lack of knowledge about their housing need (King and Oxley, 2000).

Political acceptability

A further common argument, at least historically, has been that housing consumption is politically acceptable, whereas a cash payment, which could be used for such things as alcohol and tobacco, might not be. As a society we approve of certain activities as being legitimate for subsidy, but not others. Thus we should ensure that public money is spent on things that benefit individuals and not merely on wants and desires.

But were we to accept this argument we would offer no cash benefits whatsoever and merely provide clothing vouchers, food parcels and so on to those who were not well off. Clearly society feels comfortable providing benefits and pensions for its citizens and feels sanguine about their competence to spend the money wisely. We might therefore argue that the same ought to apply to housing if individuals are capable of making decisions for themselves about how they spend their income.

We can point to a linked argument, which states that it is not fair to allow people on low incomes to make choices that can affect them disproportionately when compared with those on reasonable incomes. Thus to give individuals a housing allowance and tell them to pay their rent, as well as food, transport and fuel bills, is to set them up to fail. Therefore, the argument runs, it is better to provide houses rather than housing allowances.

The heart of this issue is whether housing is any different from other goods and services. Clearly, as we saw in our discussion on market failure in chapter 3, there are some differences, particularly the cost of housing and its immobility. Yet this is partially offset by the ability that most people have to understand their own housing needs.

Links to wider social and political problems

Another argument is that poor quality housing can lead to wider societal problems, such as ill health, vandalism, racism, family break-up, etc. If people live in poor quality housing they may become ill, or if there is a shortage of suitable housing in an area, it might stir up racial tensions if some groups believe they are being excluded and others given preferential treatment. The point is that housing can have far-reaching effects, which go beyond fulfilling the wants of individual households. Housing provision, or the lack of it, can have social effects and it is difficult for individuals to deal with these problems themselves. Therefore it is suggested that building more social housing and to a high standard can help to deal with these social problems.

Yet this argument only works if there are no resulting social problems in social housing. Unfortunately this is not the case and many social housing estates have proven to be centres of economic dependency, anti-social behaviour and poverty. On one level we should expect this as social housing is allocated on the basis of need, so that those without work and with no alternatives are most likely to become tenants.

Cost differentials

A more technical argument for object subsidies is that, because of the differences in land and property values across the country, there are differential costs in a rental market, and these can be ironed out by the provision of social housing at controlled rent levels. This relates to the point discussed above regarding government's ability to ensure a comprehensive and uniform coverage across the country. By subsidising the production of social housing, even if it means paying higher levels of subsidy to landlords in high cost areas, rents can be similar across the country. This, it is argued, can encourage labour mobility, as well as being seen to be fair and just.

This argument would only be valid if social housing were free or available at very low rents so that cost was not an issue at all for any household. But this would suggest that object subsidies would need to be considerably higher per dwelling than has historically been the case, and that social landlords should receive a higher level of continuing revenue subsidy to assist them in managing and maintaining their stock of dwellings.

But, of course, there is no reason why the logic of differential costs cannot apply to a housing allowance system (King, 2006). The current Housing Benefit system in the UK is, in most cases, based on actual rents and thus payments differ between high and low rent areas. The net effect of this on household access is no different from that of paying different levels of subsidy to allow landlords to build in these areas. So there is nothing intrinsic to object subsidies that assists with cost differentials.

Benefit take-up

It can be argued that, as the take-up for a housing allowance will inevitably be below 100 per cent, some people will miss out on what they are entitled to. This might be because some people are unaware of their entitlements, or because they perceive a stigma attached to handouts from the state. Thus it might be best to fund housing providers to ensure that good quality housing is available without the need for households to claim benefits.

Of course, this argument presupposes that the knowledge of the availability of social housing is at a higher level than that of welfare benefits, as well as an assumption that a person who is unaware of one form of subsidy would be aware of another.

Poverty trap

A problem associated with subject subsidies is that they can create a poverty trap because individuals are reluctant to take low paid work because of the way in which their benefits are withdrawn as their income rises. For instance, under current Housing Benefit regulations in the UK, 65 pence of benefit is withdrawn for every extra pound a claimant earns. When we take into account the increasing tax and National Insurance paid as earnings increase, we can see how someone might be better off on benefit rather than working. It can therefore be argued that providing the goods 'in kind', in the form of social housing, would help to deal with this problem.

But this assumes that rents are low enough to ensure access to those on very low incomes. In practice, in the UK and elsewhere, a majority of social housing tenants can only afford their housing because they receive a subject subsidy. We might also question what impact zero or very low rents would have on incentives: why give up a good that is free, even if our income rises considerably?

Controlling subsidies

One great advantage of object subsidies, for government if no one else, is that they can allow for greater control over the quality of housing provided for low income households. By providing subsidies to a particular level and applying a particular control and monitoring regime, government can ensure a high quality of outcomes. Conversely, it can also ensure that recipients do not benefit excessively from public funds. A key problem with housing allowance systems is that government finds it hard to control the number of recipients and rent levels and therefore the level of expenditure. Government can limit entitlements and eligibility, but this is less fine-grained than the control it can have over object subsidies where it can much more accurately set the limits of funding.

This is the reason, of course, why successive governments have not totally abandoned object subsidies. But, whilst some might consider this a strong argument, we can question whether controlling systems is sufficient justification for a form of subsidy. The purpose of subsidies is not to allow government to control social landlords, but to assist certain households deemed to be in need. At best this can therefore only be a subsidiary argument and not something that should be seen as the basis for keeping one system or another. Indeed, if control were the sole basis for housing subsidies, we could surely come up with a housing allowance system that disbursed a pre-determined number of vouchers operated through a needs-based allocation system. But this is again not what we consider housing subsidies are designed to do. We return to this issue in more detail in chapter 6.

Incentives to build

A final argument in favour of object subsidies is that they act as direct incentives to supply new housing. It was argued that if we have a shortage of housing, as was the case in most Western countries throughout the twentieth century, subsidising landlords is the most direct and effective way of getting houses built. But it also encourages quality by allowing landlords to build to a higher standard than they otherwise would. If left to a market they would perhaps be more concerned with covering their costs and making a profit based on the limitations of the budgets of the households to whom the houses would be let.

Of course, this presupposes that government is capable of planning effectively so that housing is in the right place and of the right price and quality. Yet, as we have seen already, many low income households can only afford access to social housing if they receive an additional subject subsidy.

Arguments for subject subsidies

This final point, which we have made several times now, leads us to consider subject subsidies. Social housing is only accessible to some households if they receive an additional subsidy and this might indicate that object subsidies do not work as intended. Of course, this does not mean that subject subsidies are automatically to be preferred. It may well be that overall they pose bigger problems to the creation of an effective system of housing supports. Yet, before we can judge, we need to explore the main justifications for them.

Producer capture

It is assumed that the purpose of subsidies is to help people in need. Yet on several occasions we have suggested that subsidies are also used to control provision. The question we therefore need to consider is whom or what are subsidy systems for, and do they benefit the producers of the service or the consumers (King, 1998)? It can be argued that object subsidies can be controlled by producers and operate to their benefit. If producers can control subsidies – because they receive them – how can we ensure that consumers are being treated properly and that provision is being made efficiently and fairly?

One way of examining this issue is through the arguments of *public choice theory*. Boyne *et al.* (2003) suggest that public choice theory is based upon three main criticisms of the role of public organisations. First, they suggest that many public services are provided by monopoly suppliers, either at the national level, such as the NHS, or locally, such as local authority housing departments. Public monopoly can lead to poor performance because officials have little incentive to keep costs down or innovate. There are few financial or other benefits for those who innovate and resources are not directed by the users but by a 'political' sponsor. Therefore officials are more likely to respond to political pressure than to that from customers.

Second, there is an absence of valid indicators of organisational performance by which to judge outcomes and ensure consumers' interests are uppermost. Public choice theorists suggest that there are no unambiguous indicators in the public sector, such as profit and loss, making it difficult to evaluate individual or collective performance. Third, the large size of public organisations creates problems of co-ordination and control, and these lead to a decline in performance as the size of the organisation increases. In response to these issues public choice theorists advocate a more competitive structure, with rivalries within the public sector and between public and private sectors. This would force greater information sharing to enable performance to be judged and would break up large agencies into smaller units (Boyne *et al.*, 2003). They also suggest that consumers be given some level of choice in determining their supplier and the level of service they receive. The most direct manner of achieving this is through the use of vouchers for services or by directing subsidies to the consumers themselves, thereby forcing producers to compete for their custom.

However, we need to appreciate that subject subsidies are not necessarily immune to producer capture, and the UK Housing Benefit system is an example of this. So long as private and social housing providers were able to set their own rents they were able to use Housing Benefit as a further form of revenue subsidy. This is because of the heavy dependence on Housing Benefit on the part of tenants and the method of payment, which is made direct to landlords so that tenants have been largely unaffected by, and unaware of, changes in rent levels. In addition, the system has allowed for some tenants to claim their full rent. The reforms to the Housing Benefit system that were introduced in 2008[1] were intended to deal with this, and this suggests that the problem here is one of system design. Thus it is possible to design a housing allowance system not prone to producer capture. However, it is difficult to imagine a system of object subsidies that would be so immune, as by definition they involve providing financial support to organisations.

Targeting

One of the main justifications for subject subsidies is that they can be targeted at those in need and can be withdrawn when income increases. Households who are allocated social housing can stay there all their lives, regardless of how their income and personal circumstances change. Thus needy low income households might be denied access to social housing because more affluent households remain in occupation, even though they might now be able to afford owner occupation or private renting. A system of subject subsidies, however, could prevent this because households are subsidised according to their current, and not their past, circumstances. The subsidy can thus be withdrawn if and when their circumstances change.

There has been some discussion in both England and the Netherlands about time-limited social tenancies and so making them as means tested as housing allowances. This is still, however, a controversial proposal with some people suggesting it will merely worsen the problem of social polarisation in social housing, in that economic dependency will effectively become a condition for maintaining a tenancy. There might also be problems with moral hazard in that tenants would have an incentive to remain economically dependent in order to keep their social tenancy.

Increase in tenants' negotiating strength

It could be argued that object subsidies give too dominant a role to landlords at the expense of tenants. Landlords are able to exercise control over rents and the level of service offered to tenants. However, paying subsidies to tenants gives them some negotiating strength in relation to rent levels. It would create a different and more equal relationship between landlord and tenant. In principle a system of housing vouchers, which operates in some parts of the USA, allows for this situation. However, in practice it does depend on the co-operation of landlords and their preparedness to accept low income tenants with vouchers.

Tenure neutrality

A further advantage claimed for subject subsidies is that they can be tenure neutral, in that they can be applied to all housing sectors, including, if so desired, owner occupation. Subject subsidy systems can be devised that are so designed as to allow access to all and can be dependent only on income rather than tenure or any particular relationship with the state.

No links between subsidies and quality

Whilst the supporters of object subsidies argue that it helps landlords to build good quality housing, there is no automatic link between this form of subsidy and quality outputs (even where there is sufficient demand for the dwellings). Social landlords have been guilty of building poor quality and unpopular housing (Page, 1993; Power, 1987, 1993). Many social landlords were encouraged by the subsidy system in the 1950s and 1960s to build high-rise blocks (Power, 1987), which are not universally popular and, as with the example of Ronan Point in London, which collapsed in 1968, have proved on occasions to be disastrous.

Unbalanced communities

Developing this point on the nature of the outcomes of state provision, it can be argued that object subsidies have led to ghettoisation and unbalanced communities (Marsland, 1996). The system has created large estates where many of the occupants are economically inactive and where those who can afford to leave do so. As a result, social housing has become a key indicator of social exclusion.

However, in mitigation, the point that most of these tenants, in the UK at least, are also in receipt of housing allowances suggests that the subject subsidies are not immune to this problem either. We might actually say here that the problem of unbalanced communities is precisely a result of the combination of social housing and welfare benefits, rather than one or the other.

Choice

Perhaps the most significant benefit to be derived from a subject subsidy system is that it can offer households some choice over where they live and the type of accommodation they wish to reside in. Paying the subsidy directly to households enables them to exercise more control over their lives than if the subsidy were paid to landlords who built what they felt was required where it was needed. As we have seen several times already, the issue of system design is crucial here, as in Britain much of the Housing Benefit paid out goes directly to the landlord, which detracts from this particular advantage of subject subsidies. But this is not a necessary part of the system and could be remedied by a change in policy.

Paying benefit directly to individual households enables them to have some choice over their housing, which is not open to households in an object subsidy system. Of course, this does not mean that households have an untrammelled choice or that their options are limitless. This is used as a criticism of choice-based systems, in that because choice is not limitless, and indeed in practice might be quite restricted, it is somehow an illusion. Yet the choices open to all households, even to an extent the wealthy, are limited, being hemmed in by income and family ties, employment opportunities, available schools and the quality of public transport; this is before we even consider such issues as housing supply and availability. What we have to remember is that choice does not have to be limitless still to be choice.

In some ways this is a rather redundant debate because most governments seem to favour subject subsidies. This may, however, change in the future and the problems in housing markets in 2007/2008 and onwards have generated calls for an increase in social housing production in expectation of an increase in demand. But this call may go unheeded, partly due to cost, but also to the now-ingrained support for owner occupation and the ideology of choice (King, 2006).

We should also beware of seeing the debate in purely oppositional terms. It is not the case of *either* object or subject subsidies, but rather the *balance* between them. Whilst some countries have abolished object subsidies entirely, it is still common for there to be hybrid systems that incorporate both forms of subsidy, even to the extent that the same household may be eligible for both.

However, the debate about types of subsidy is important because it demonstrates what government intervention exists to do and how government seeks to go about it. It exhibits, therefore, the practical limits of government action, about what it is possible to do and what impact it has. Where this debate becomes most emotive is over the direct provision of housing by government. We have suggested that this form of intervention is in decline, with a greater emphasis being placed on housing allowances. Yet it is social housing that is the most demonstrable form of government action and, in principle, the most practical: providing houses is ostensibly a very straightforward means of dealing with a housing shortage. We therefore need to look, albeit briefly, at the direct provision of social housing and, in particular, what it is for.

Think point

Which of the arguments for object and subject subsidies do you find the most compelling? Give reasons for your answer and try to find a relevant example.

What is social housing for?

Social housing has been the mainstay of provision for low income households in the UK since the early part of the twentieth century. It has not provided for all such households, indeed it is clear that until 1972 the very poorest were excluded (King, 2006; Malpass, 1990). Yet it was clearly intended to help those who could not find good quality housing through markets.

However, the shift towards subject subsidies puts the role of social housing into question, and indeed this role has been openly questioned in Britain, particularly with the publication of the Hills report on the future of social housing in 2007 (Hills, 2007). This was a government commissioned review of the role of social housing within the context of growing demand for owner occupation. Therefore, it could be seen as an attempt to either justify social housing or consign it to history as an anachronism.

The outcome of the Hills review was that social housing was still justified and that its advantages, in terms of increased quality, affordability, avoidance of discrimination and polarisation, outweighed the disadvantages of rationing a scarce resource and the problems of differential market conditions across the country (Hills, 2007). The list of advantages presented by Hills is similar to the arguments for object subsidies discussed above, and so it is clear that Hills came out in support of continued social provision, albeit with the provision of more flexible routes into housing, such as shared ownership.

Perhaps the most significant issue surrounding the Hills report, however, was that government actually felt the need to commission it, and that therefore the very notion of social provision in the future was being questioned. This would have been unthinkable a generation earlier, but now it seemed that government was openly seeking some justification for social housing in the twenty-first century.

In the light of this, we ought to look at what role social housing purports to have. My aim here is not to look at social housing historically, as this would have to be a very long section if I tried to look at a number of countries. Those who wish to pursue the history further might turn to Power (1987) and Malpass (2005) for a survey of British social housing, and to Harloe (1995) and Power (1993) for a comparative perspective. What I want to do is look at what role social housing is meant to play in general terms. But in doing so it allows us to pick out international differences, for example, that social housing need not signify state ownership (as was historically the case in Britain) but refer rather to a client group or how it is funded (as is more common in Europe). In this section I want to identify three ways in which we can define the purpose of social housing (see Table 4.5).

Table 4.5   Three ways of defining social housing

• Whom it is for.
• Who owns it.
• Who pays for it.

First, we can define social housing in terms of *what it is for*. Typically, this would be where we see need or vulnerability as the main justification for the provision of housing by government, as well as for its allocation. If we concern ourselves with the purpose of social housing, what matters, therefore, is access and who gets into the dwellings.

Second, we can define social housing in terms of *who owns it*. This particularly pertains to countries like the UK and Ireland, which built up large stocks of social housing over much of the twentieth century. In the UK the issue of ownership has been very important in defining social housing, with the idea of local political accountability being held very strongly, at least until the late 1990s. We can see this in the debate over the Right to Buy, which involved the sale at a discount of over 2.2 million dwellings (a third of the total stock) to sitting tenants. This was seen by some as a form of privatisation and a denuding of a national asset for private gain.

More recently the situation has become more complicated and not just because of the effects of the Right to Buy. Since the early 1990s over a million dwellings have been transferred to either new or existing housing associations, and this has sat alongside a policy of all new social housing being built by housing associations. Therefore social housing in the UK is no longer council housing and the issue of being owned by the state is now less relevant.

The third means of defining social housing is through *who pays for it*. Housing can be defined as social if it is funded by government with the aim of achieving some particular purpose. So we might take the use of government subsidies as a defining characteristic. However, we have seen that object subsidies are diminishing, with a greater emphasis on subject subsidies paid to individuals. In addition, as we shall see in chapter 6, there has been an increased reliance on private finance to fund and maintain social housing. This then calls into question finance as an indicator of social housing. Indeed, would we want to define housing as social because government allowed tax relief on mortgage interest?

Perhaps, then, the most useful definition relates to whom social housing is for rather than who owns it or how it is funded. Social housing aims to provide good quality housing to those who cannot provide it for themselves through a market. We can suggest that this means that social housing exists as a form of solidarity. Related to this, we can perhaps argue that social housing seeks to remedy social divisions by putting all households on a more equal footing. Therefore government intervenes in markets to ensure all people are well housed, and historically has chosen the direct provision of housing in order to achieve this aim.

However, this purpose is now increasingly becoming a historical one. Social housing may be the most visible example of government intervention in housing markets, but it is becoming something of an anachronism as governments choose other means of acting. In the discussion on types of subsidies we pointed to some of the possible reasons for this, which included a shift in the dominant ideology towards a more market-oriented position and the fact that object subsidies could not be so precisely targeted. But a further reason might be that direct provision fails. Just as we could point to market failure, might not there be such a thing as government failure? In the discussion on producer capture above we introduced the idea that state provision might be taken over by other interests so that it stops being entirely about social solidarity and becomes more about protecting producer interests. So does government fail just as markets do?

Do subsidies mean sustainable housing?

In the 1970s John Turner, an architect, wrote about the attempts of households in Latin America to provide housing for themselves. He wanted to show that government intervention is not always helpful and that instead households and communities are often better able to provide for themselves if they are just given the right resources and the space to use them. In his book *Housing by People* (1976) he articulates two case studies carried out in Mexico City in 1971. He compares the temporary shack of a young rag-picker and his family with that of a modern, government subsidised dwelling lived in by a semi-employed middle-aged mason and his family.

The dwelling of the rag-picker and his family is literally a shack of corrugated iron and wood located in the backyard of a family member's house. It has very basic amenities, yet Turner argues it is supportive. It is near to the family's source of income, close to family and friends, and cheap enough to allow them to survive with the hope of obtaining a better dwelling as their prospects improve. It thus offers them considerable freedom and Turner therefore refers to it as the 'supportive shack' (1976, p. 54). It is very basic accommodation, yet it fulfils the family's immediate needs and allows them to control their environment.

The dwelling of the mason's family is a modern house in a purpose-built estate paid for by government subsidy. However, it is located away from the family's network of friends and, crucially, away from the mason's place of employment. The mason pays out 5 per cent of his income in transport costs to and from work, in addition to the 55 per cent spent on rent and utility charges. Moreover, his wife had previously run a small vending business from their previous dwelling, which was now forbidden under the tenancy regulations. Thus their income has been reduced as their housing and transport costs have risen. Turner refers to this case as the 'oppressive house' (1976, p. 56). Thus an improvement in material standards can be counterproductive because, being based on abstract standards, they cannot take into account the particular needs and conditions of the household. Turner thus concludes from these cases that material standards are not necessarily the most useful measure. He states, 'Some of the poorest dwellings, materially speaking, were clearly the best, socially speaking, and some, but not all of the highest standard dwellings, were the most socially aggressive' (1976, p. 52).

Turner argues that the use of government subsidies does not necessarily lead to a material improvement in the lives of people. For him the problem is the wrong set of values imposed by government. These values are economic and based on material standards. Turner instead argues for what he calls human values, which emphasise the use to which they can be put and the level of control that the household can exercise over their immediate environment (King, 1996). This necessitates access to resources, but these should be on the terms of the household and the local community rather than those of central government.

We might see this as just one example, and in any case it comes from the developing world and so does not apply to large industrial societies like the USA or the UK. But Turner states that the same displaced values apply also in the developed world. The difference is rather one of scale and cost, in that richer countries have gone further down the road of mass government provision.

We can argue over Turner's point and whether his view on government intervention is correct. However, what his example does show is the possibility that even the best laid plans can go wrong. This might be seen as the other side of the invisible hand we discussed in chapter 3. We suggested that markets act to achieve outcomes without any individual or agency expressing a particular intention. We noted that things turn out unexpectedly, and this does not only apply to markets; we can also see this occurring in the case of government intervention.

Unintended consequences

An unintended consequence is when an outcome occurs that was not expressly part of the intentions of policy makers. It is when outcomes were not foreseen and thus could not be taken into account in the policy process. We can suggest that these occur, in housing as elsewhere, because systems are both *open* and *dynamic*. We cannot contain a particular housing tenure, or type of organisation, or even households from external influence. The different tenures interact, as we shall consider in chapters 5 and 6, and housing systems are open to external influence through the linkage of housing to labour markets, migration patterns and the wider economy. This means that housing systems are changing constantly and are never settled. As we discussed in chapter 3, problems in the sub-prime mortgage market in parts of the USA has had an impact across the world, affecting housing markets, changing the perceptions and expectations of households and forcing governments into emergency actions, such as the nationalisation of several banks in the UK, the USA and Europe.

This being so, we can suggest that the impact of subsidies will frequently be unintended. We therefore need to come to terms with this phenomenon. Popper makes the point that:

> it is one of the striking things about social life that *nothing ever comes off exactly as intended*. Things always turn out a little bit differently. We hardly ever produce in social life precisely the effect that we wish to produce, and we usually get things that we do not want into the bargain. Of course we act with certain aims in mind; but apart from these aims (which we may or may not really achieve) there are always certain unwanted consequences of our actions; and usually these unwanted consequences cannot be eliminated.
>
> (Popper, 1989, p. 124, author's emphasis)

Popper is suggesting that unintended consequences are inevitable and cannot be avoided. All we hope to do is mitigate them by understanding the world better, by developing better theories and models of how things actually work.

This can be directly related to housing by looking at Williams's (1997) discussion on the nature of housing policy. He states that 'government might be the starting point for change but in reality policy is actually implemented by a range of organisations ... and through the actions of individual consumers' (p. 2). Government, as we have suggested, has to rely on others for the implementation of policy. As a result the process is much more complicated than if government could exercise total control. But this means that:

> we still do not fully understand the interactions between different elements or the ways these combine in different ways in different settings. As a result policy, however well conceived, can have major unintended consequences, worsening the position and forcing yet more policy interventions.
>
> (Williams, 1997, p. 2)

Williams sees unintended consequences as a matter of not knowing enough about the interrelationships that occur in a complex social order. It is not that government is not competent, but that it has not proved capable *yet*. Williams is not questioning the ability of policy makers to formulate the correct policies eventually, so he does not concur with Popper's more general argument that unintended consequences are inevitable. For Williams the problem of unintended consequences is a result of the system not operating properly, with the clear implication that with greater knowledge – with more research and analysis – it could be made to do so.

The problem with Williams's argument, however, is that there is no evidence that such a high state of knowledge will ever be reached. Indeed it is more plausible to argue that it is simply not possible to rid a system of unintended consequences. This is not because policy makers and researchers currently do not know enough, but because they can *never* do so. If we assume the current level of complexity within economic systems, and the existing diversity of interests and subjective expectations of millions of individuals and organisations, how can we model a complex social order with any accuracy? The problem, therefore, is not one of unintended consequences, but the belief that we are capable of pre-empting them.

This may lead to a rather pessimistic conclusion, namely, that if we cannot pre-empt the unintended, why should we bother making policy at all? But we could apply this same logic to markets: if we cannot predict market outcomes, why take part in them? The answer to both questions is the same: we have no choice. Markets exist and so does government and we can expect neither to go away. We therefore have to engage with what is in front of us and act accordingly. And what will help us is some scepticism about both markets and government and some expectation that the unexpected will occur.

Think point

If government action does not succeed in its aims can we still justify it? What alternatives are there?

Conclusions

Government action is a fact of life. It is pervasive and has helped shape housing systems in a fundamental way. We might suggest that the history of housing over the last century is really the history of government subsidies. Yet, as we have seen, this does not mean that government action is always successful or that different types of action do not have radically different effects.

Government action is directed at markets and we now have some understanding of both. We can now move on to look at some concrete examples of how housing systems work and the roles taken by markets and government in creating and maintaining these systems. In the next two chapters we shall consider how government seeks to influence markets (chapter 5) and how it uses financial mechanisms to control housing provision (chapter 6). We shall try to develop a narrative here of the role of housing finance within the dynamic relationship between markets and government. In particular, we shall show a shift from explicit government intervention to deal with market failure to an attempt by government to reform public provision through the use of market disciplines. We shall attempt to explain this development and understand what this means for housing finance.

Further reading

It is fair to say that most books on housing policy focus on the role of the state and its impact – after all, housing policy is what government does. However, a good, long-term overview is provided by Peter Malpass in his book *Housing and the Welfare State* (2005). A critical look at the role of government in housing can be found in my books *Housing, Individuals and the State* (1998) and *Choice and the End of Social Housing* (2006). The issue of housing subsidies is debated in depth in King and Oxley's *Housing: Who Decides?* (2000).

5

Influencing markets

Learning outcomes

- How government tries to influence market outcomes.
- Why owner occupation is so politically and economically important.
- The impact of rent controls.
- The use and effect of housing allowances.
- The complexity of relations between markets and government.

Introduction

In 1999 the Blair government proposed a reform of the process of buying and selling houses in England. The aim was to make the housing market work better by speeding up the process, introducing more certainty and dealing with the problem of gazumping, whereby a buyer would find themselves outbid at the last minute and after they had thought the seller was committed to selling to them. The proposal was for a *Home Information Pack* (HIP) to be prepared by the seller of a dwelling, which would include a structural survey, as well as the property search, deeds, etc. It would include, therefore, all the information a buyer would need and it would only have to be provided once instead of a survey being commissioned by anyone considering a purchase.

As the process was getting underway, the European Union introduced a directive that all dwellings should have an energy rating in an attempt to improve energy efficiency. Accordingly, a requirement for an energy certificate was included in the HIP. After a pilot of the system and a lot of delay the government announced that HIPs would become compulsory from

June 2007, but only after the requirement for a structural survey had been removed to simplify the process. The main justification from the government now concerned energy efficiency and the need to deal with climate change. In readiness for the June 2007 start surveyors and others had committed to becoming qualified HIPs assessors, many at their own expense. It was seen as a secure form of income, as it was estimated that a HIP would cost between £300 and £600.

But the fact that the major requirement – the structural survey – had been removed made some query its usefulness. In addition, there were apparently not yet enough trained assessors. This led the government to temporarily delay its introduction for six weeks and to exclude properties of fewer than four bedrooms, and make it necessary only that a HIP be ordered, but not necessarily completed, before a house was put up for sale. Later in 2007 the requirement for a HIP was extended to all dwellings, but the plan to ensure sellers had a HIP before putting the property up for sale was again delayed.

The problem with HIPs was that it was actually slowing down the market by creating an extra obstacle, as well as increasing the transaction costs of moving house. It was felt that the additional cost would put off so-called speculative transactions – when households put their property up for sale to test its value but then carried on to sell. Perhaps, more fundamentally, it became clear that no potential buyer would simply trust the information in the pack and, of course, the potential purchaser still needed to commission a survey at their own expense. The claim of many estate agents was that HIPs were seldom looked at by potential buyers anyway.

Of course, what made the extra cost imposed by HIPs look particularly ill-judged was the fact that in late 2007 the housing market took a downward turn, with a reduction in market activity and a fall in prices. The last thing that sellers needed was the additional cost of HIPs and the extra bureaucracy it entailed just at a time when it was becoming much harder to sell their dwelling anyway.

So, in hindsight, we can see HIPs as a mistake. It was a policy that arose out of good intentions – to speed up the housing market and reduce uncertainty – but that actually has had the reverse effect. Yet what has also become clear is that government is not prepared to repeal the legislation. Despite it being so obvious that the policy was ill-conceived and unhelpful, ministers continue with the fiction that it is useful and that it should stay. Of course, politicians are notoriously shy of admitting error or of apologising, and to repeal HIPs would indeed offer proof that the policy was a failure and would call into question the competence of ministers.

What this example shows, and why it is relevant to our discussion on housing finance, is the very real difficulties government faces when intervening in markets. Despite good intentions, HIPs have had the reverse effect intended and are manifestly a waste of time and money. We can suggest that the reason is because government could not foresee how consumers would react and, of course, how markets would change in the future. The change in consumer behaviour might have been predicted, but certainly the change in global economic circumstances could not have been foreseen. The HIPs saga shows just how complex market relations are. But it also points to the impact of politics, when the costs of repealing a failed policy are still seen as being greater than the benefits of putting it right. We might see this as a microcosm of the relationship between markets and government, with well-intentioned policies going wrong, yet being very hard to remedy.

This is what we shall be considering in this chapter: how government tries to influence markets and what happens as a result. We have looked at subsidies and what social housing is for. Now we need to look at how government has actually influenced markets. We shall be looking at three distinct areas of housing finance policy.

First, we shall continue to explore owner occupation and look at how government has intervened not only to promote the tenure, but also to moderate some of the fluctuations in the market. In doing so, we shall explore some of the peculiarities of owner occupation that help to explain why it is so significant economically and politically.

Second, we shall consider the issue of rent control and how government has tried to influence rent levels in the private sector. We shall also explore what happened in England when statutory rent controls were lifted in 1989, and how government found it necessary to reintroduce new controls within only a few years, albeit of a more administrative and non-statutory kind. The reason for this was the existence of a comprehensive system of rent allowances, which meant that landlords could increase rents towards market levels without it impinging dramatically on tenants, who could rely on Housing Benefit to take the strain. This meant, of course, that the cost of increased rents was borne by government itself.

Therefore it is not a coincidence that the third issue we shall consider is that of housing allowances. The issue of means testing and its effects will be explored, as well as the ability of landlords to control housing allowances, which is a particular problem with the Housing Benefit system in the UK. We shall look at attempts to reform the Housing Benefit system and show that this resonates strongly with some of the conceptual discussions in chapter 2, particularly on choice and responsibility.

Despite possible appearances to the contrary, it is not my particular intention to be critical of government, and certainly not to indulge in any polemic. I do not wish to argue for any particular level of government involvement. I have already stated that government action is ubiquitous, and we cannot know what would have happened if government had not intervened.

Hypothetical situations can always be made to look better than actual ones and this is because in theory policies have no faults, whilst in practice they may have many. I do not, then, wish to argue that government intervention into markets is always mistaken or that it will necessarily fail. Rather, what I want to show is the complexity of the relationships within and between markets and government, and how factors link together, but in ways that are unpredictable and not straightforward. I want to show the cross-over effects caused by dynamic systems that are open to external influence. Government has to cope with this situation when it intervenes but it always struggles to do so because it is unable – as we all are – to see into the future. We need to remember that all evidence, all data, are historical; they only ever tell us anything definite about the past (Mises, 1996).

My argument is based on the assertion that governments seek to do two things. First, government attempts to *influence markets*, which it may do for a number of reasons, but, in general, we can accept it is to ensure that all citizens have access to high quality affordable housing. Second, government tries to *control provision*, in order to meet its own objectives and so that its effects are proportionate, and its costs and liabilities are managed and controlled. I wish to argue that all housing finance mechanisms serve either one purpose or both. We can differentiate between them by seeing one as an explicit purpose – influencing markets – and the other, implicit – control. Hence one aim tends to be stated openly, whilst the other is not.

It may also be that one follows the other, in that we might contend that control follows attempts to influence. This may be because of cross-over effects and unintended consequences, because a policy has gone wrong or is now having an unwanted effect. Hence government now believes that the policy has to be moderated or certain agencies or interests have to be held in check. This is why we are looking at the influence on markets in this chapter before analysing the issue of control of policy in chapter 6.

In chapter 7, which concludes this book, I make some comments about the role of government and markets and the balance between them. Without completely pre-empting the argument in that chapter, my conclusion concerning the relationship between markets and government action is that much of such action will inevitably be *reactive*, and that this applies even when government is claiming to plan ahead or to be exercising 'joined-up' thinking. As a result, government will only ever be partially informed and so its action will remain prone to unintended consequences. The reason for this is not because of problems intrinsic to government so much as the nature of markets. This is partly because markets are international and so beyond the scope and control of any one government. But, more fundamentally, it is because markets have no purpose and, as such, cannot be planned for with any certainty. Markets are not ends in themselves but means in which the needs and wants of individuals and organisations can be met. They are not directed and nor are they directable. This means that government cannot pre-empt a market, but merely react to conditions as they develop. The discussion in this chapter and the two that follow is aimed at substantiating this hypothesis.

The overriding political importance of owner occupation

Owner occupation is portrayed as the tenure of choice, and when we talk about the housing market, we generally mean owner occupation. Of course, in many countries there is a large and vibrant private rented market, offering a range of accommodation of widely differing price and quality. But what tends to create both economic and political waves is the fact that in many European countries as well as the so-called Anglosphere world,[1] owner occupation is now the dominant tenure and the tenure that most households expect and aspire to.

The economic downturn of 2007 and 2008 made this very clear, with the problems of the sub-prime mortgage market in the USA and the subsequent credit crunch. In late 2007 Northern Rock, Britain's third-largest mortgage lender, found itself unable to obtain funds to refinance its loans portfolio, despite its apparently sound balance sheet. In response to this the Bank of England provided upwards of £60 billion to Northern Rock to enable it to continue trading and to guarantee the savings of its depositors. Subsequently, because no private buyer could be found for the stricken bank, it was nationalised in 2008. To put the scale of the government's commitment into context, £60 billion would fund the entire UK Housing Benefit budget for four full years, or would pay for all of the social housing development programmes in England, Scotland and Wales for nearly eight years.

As the scale of the financial crisis deepened, the UK government, as well as those in the USA, France, Germany and other European countries, took many of their larger mortgage lenders into complete or partial public ownership. The UK government, for example, spent £37 billion to buy shares in three high street banks and offered guarantees of up to £500 billion. This latter figure equates to over 80 per cent of annual government expenditure.

These figures demonstrate the political – and electoral – importance of owner occupation in countries like Britain and the USA. Indeed, it is so significant that government cannot afford to leave it alone. When 70 per cent of households are owner occupiers, what happens to housing markets is a matter of concern to government. But also, because of the size of the tenure and the fact that housing is typically the largest item in a household's budget, government is aware that it can affect consumer behaviour through the manipulation of housing costs. Government, like that of the UK in the early 1990s, can use its ability to control interest rates to affect mortgage costs with the aim of reducing consumer spending and thereby reducing inflationary pressures on the economy (King, 1996).

But, it might be argued, the reason that owner occupation is so popular is because it is supported by government. Whilst politicians tend to do things they think will be popular, things tend to increase in popularity if they are subsidised by government. Unravelling this situation – is owner occupation popular because it has been subsidised, or is it subsidised because it is popular? – is virtually impossible. However, in the UK, government support for owner occupation has reduced since the early 1990s without any great reduction in the perceived popularity of the tenure.

The popular conception of the politics of owner occupation that used to hold can be summed up by a rather old (and bad) joke:

Husband: Well, that's the mortgage paid off.
Wife: Thank goodness for that – now we can vote Labour again!

The belief was that increasing owner occupation would encourage people to vote Conservative. This was because only the Conservatives could be trusted to support owner occupiers, whilst the Labour party was wedded to its policy of supporting social housing.

The Thatcher government appeared to believe there was a positive link between voting Conservative and owner occupation when it proclaimed its aim of creating a 'property owning democracy'. There has been considerable academic debate about whether there is a link between voting and tenure (Saunders, 1990). The Conservative themselves, on the basis of the vigour with which they supported owner occupation, clearly believed that there was just such a link.

But the support for owner occupation is no longer limited to one party. No serious political party in the UK can oppose the tenure. This might be because of populism: owner occupation is the preferred tenure, even for social housing tenants, and governments of left or right have to respond to this. But, as we summarise in Table 5.1 and discuss more fully below, there are actually a number of reasons for governments' interest in owner occupation that have more to do with economics than political popularity.

Table 5.1   The political importance of owner occupation

• Its effect on consumption.
• Derived demand from buying and selling houses.
• House construction is labour intensive.
• The cost of housing diverges considerably from house values.
• The final cost of housing is unknown until the last mortgage payment is made.

Housing as a consumption good

As we have suggested, housing costs are usually the largest single item in any household's budget. This means that changes in housing costs are likely to have considerable effects on total household consumption. A general increase in housing costs, through an increase in the costs of borrowing, has major economic effects through reducing general consumption. Importantly, these effects go beyond housing and affect demand in other markets, as households have less disposable income after housing costs. An increase in mortgage costs reduces the income a household has to spend on other activities, like holidays, motoring and new electronic and white goods, etc.

A further effect of owner occupation is the so-called *cascade effect*, whereby housing wealth is passed from the one generation to the next. Most children will inherit the property of their parents and this effectively liquidates the wealth stored in the property. This means that the wealth of a significant number of households, most of whom are already owner occupiers, is further enhanced. This may well mean that they consume more housing and the demand for larger dwellings increases. Thus the wealth generated by owner occupation tends to become polarised, with some households quite asset rich as a result of inheritance, whilst renters (who are also often following a generational pattern) miss out.

Derived demand

Owner occupation is economically important because it results in a lot of derived demand. This is market activity which arises as a result of transactions in the housing market. Many markets depend upon an active housing market, for example, the demand for DIY products, home furnishing, white goods and insurance all depend on a vibrant housing market. In addition, many solicitors depend on their conveyancing business and estate agents are particularly susceptible to changes in the market as they rely entirely on the level of sales. A boom or slump in the housing market has considerable spillover effects and thus owner occupation should not be taken in isolation.

Labour intensive industry

Another important point is that housebuilding has traditionally been seen as a means of boosting economic activity. This is because, as in all areas of construction, housebuilding is labour intensive and not particularly import sensitive. Thus an active housing market, which encourages new development, can have a positive effect on local labour markets.

The divergence of cost and value

Because of the way in which housing is financed, there may often be a significant divergence between a household's regular costs (i.e., mortgage repayments) and the value of the dwelling. This can create a considerable benefit to households in that the value of their dwelling has increased, whilst their mortgage costs have remained static. They are able to tap into the free equity of their property to fund additional expenditure. This is known as *equity withdrawal*. This will have the effect of increasing consumption and might help to boost economic activity. However, in other circumstances it might be inflationary.

But this divergence between cost and value can also work in the opposite way. In 1992 there were 1.77 million households, mainly in England, for whom the value of their property was less than their mortgage. This *negative equity* meant that they could not sell their dwelling without making a loss. This problem is often compounded by the fact that, as housing costs rise, perhaps due to increasing interest rates, house values decline because owner occupation becomes less attractive. Indeed, the level of interest rates has an important effect on the cost of housing, which operates independently of the initial cost of purchasing the dwelling.

One of the most important factors is when the property was purchased. It is perfectly possible for one household to be paying twice as much as their neighbour for a similar property. This is simply because of when they bought it. If a household took out a mortgage of £50,000 to purchase the average house in 1990, then they are still making repayments based on that cost, even though the value of that average house in 2008 might be £200,000. But anyone purchasing the average dwelling in 2008 would be expected to repay a mortgage based on a property valuation of £200,000 plus.

The unknown cost of housing

The fact that housing costs change over time highlights another important facet of owner occupation. Not only is a property the most expensive item we are ever likely to buy, it is also the only commodity we will purchase without knowledge of its final cost. This is because factors such as interest rates and government policy might change over the life of a mortgage. Over the life of a 25-year mortgage, interest rates will have gone up and down and government policies may have changed. For instance, mortgage interest payments in the UK had been offset by tax relief. However, this tax relief was abolished in 2000, which had the effect of increasing the repayments households had to make. Individuals taking out a mortgage in 1990 would have had no means of knowing this policy change would occur. So the long-term nature of housing finance for owner occupation brings with it a degree of uncertainty and unpredictability.

Subsidies to owner occupation

Because of the political and economic significance of owner occupation, government cannot ignore it and has tended to offer financial support. However, the form of support is somewhat different from those offered to social housing. Instead of offering grants or loan guarantees, support has tended to take the form of tax relief to assist with mortgage repayments. These forms of support are often referred to as *tax expenditures*. These may be targeted on low income households, like the *Low-Income Housing Tax Credit* in the USA (Dreier, 2006), but they might also be rather less discriminating, as was the case with *mortgage interest tax relief* (MITR) in the UK and mortgage interest and property tax deductions in the USA. MITR was not made on the basis of housing need or low income, but rather was *universal*, in that all households paying tax with a mortgage were entitled to it.

MITR was finally phased out completely in April 2000. However, it had been very important to the development of owner occupation, and a source of such controversy that we still need to consider it briefly. In 1979/80, 5.9 million recipients received a total of £1,450 million, resulting in an average relief of £250 per recipient per year. In 1990/1, however, 9.6 million recipients received a total of £7,700,000 million at an average of £820 per person per year. Therefore for much of the 1990s MITR was the largest housing subsidy in the UK. Likewise, Dreier (2006) shows that in 2000 tax deductions were nearly four times as large as direct housing subsidies.

It is interesting that until 1995 and the publication of the housing White Paper of that year (DOE, 1995), the UK government did not see MITR as a housing subsidy. Indeed, with tax expenditures there is no money leaving the Treasury and being given to individuals. Rather, the government reduces the amount of tax that individuals have to pay and so they are allowed to keep more of their own money. Accordingly, government has not spent anything and so they might claim that there is no subsidy. However, the issue with tax expenditures is that this is money that would ordinarily be taken in tax and be available to spend were it not for a purposive act on the part of government. It is therefore proper to see it as having the same effect in financial and economic terms as a subsidy. However, in political terms there may be an advantage in allowing individuals to keep more of their own income rather than taking money in tax and then returning some or all of it as benefits in kind or cash.

Whilst tax expenditures are still an important feature of American housing policy, as we have seen, MITR was abolished in the UK in 2000. The level of relief had not been increased since 1983 and so had become less significant over time. But perhaps the most important factors were increased competition in the mortgage market and lower interest rates.

The most successful housing policy of all?

The most direct policy supporting the growth of owner occupation in the UK has been the Right to Buy introduced by the Conservatives in 1980. It allowed council and non-charitable housing association tenants to purchase their dwellings at a discount. The initial policy insisted on a three-year qualification period (later reduced to two years) with a maximum discount of 50 per cent (later increased to 60 per cent for flats). Both the discounts and the qualifying period have been altered since 1997 to make it less generous. However, there is no intention on the part of the Labour government to abolish it. The minority Scottish Nationalist administration elected in Scotland in 2007 has made a commitment to abolish the Right to Buy, but it is unclear as yet whether it has the political support to carry it through.

In terms of the relationships between intention and outcomes we might see the Right to Buy as being the most successful housing policy over the last 50 years. The aims of the policy were, first, to extend owner occupation to working class people, many of whom were now Conservative voters; second, to create greater independence and personal responsibility; third, to give individuals a stake in the system through owning something that could be passed on to their children; and fourth, to reduce the strength of local authorities, who at the time owned the vast majority of social housing.

On all these counts it can be said to have succeeded, in that the Conservatives retained working class support and the culture of the country altered so that property ownership became a normal and realistic expectation for most. In addition, local authorities were denuded of much of their assets and are no longer the dominant social landlords in many areas.

However, whether or not we see the Right to Buy as a success also depends on whether we take the policy in isolation. The effects of the policy have been considerable and well documented (Jones and Murie, 2006), with over 2.2 million tenants exercising their right to purchase across the UK. Of course, none of these properties was empty and available for letting, although the policy did over time reduce the ability of landlords to meet their statutory obligations. But it did not merely reduce the number of properties, it also reduced the aggregate quality of the sector, with a disproportionate number of family houses being sold, leaving unpopular flats on less desirable estates unsold.

We might say that the causes of these problems were the result of three particular elements of the policy. First, with properties being sold with a discount of at least 32 per cent, the landlord was already unable to replace them on a like-for-like basis. Second, local authorities were obliged to offer mortgages to their tenants, which therefore meant that they did not always see an immediate capital receipt. Finally, the government reclaimed outstanding subsidies from the capital receipts of sales, which further reduced any available sum. Therefore local authorities were not practically able to replace the dwelling they had been forced to sell.

Despite these problems, the most overriding issue with the Right to Buy, and what therefore shows its success as a policy, is that it is impossible to conceive of it being repealed. Even though the number of sales has declined since its peak in the 1980s, all political parties maintain support for it and so the policy remains untouchable.

The reason for this is that the Right to Buy altered the relation between an individual household and their dwelling by vesting control with the household itself. The Right to Buy focused on the use to which the household could put the dwelling. It became a personally owned asset and something the owners could pass on to their children, use as collateral, sell for a profit, take a pride in owning, etc. It therefore allowed households to exercise greater control over those things closest to them. The essence of the Right to Buy as a successful policy, therefore, was the fact that it played on the private relation between a household and their dwelling. These are the virtues that Schmidtz (1998) refers to when he discusses the internalisation of responsibility through property ownership (see chapter 2).

Think point

What are main financial advantages of owner occupation?

Economic stability and government intervention

The example of the Right to Buy shows that government will do what is popular and that this means encouraging and supporting owner occupation. This can be done with financial support, but it can also be through the broader management of the economy. Government can support the tenure by ensuring high levels of employment, maintaining stable interest rates and by keeping inflation low. What housing markets need from government is economic stability so that house prices continue to rise, but not too quickly, and so that mortgage rates stay stable and affordable. This attitude was shown in the 2000 Green Paper, released soon after MITR was abolished, which states:

> The main contribution the government can make to sustainable home-ownership is a robust economy in all parts of the country and a strong system of consumer protection. As a result of our economic policies, homeowners are benefiting from relatively low mortgage interest rates and rising living standards . . . We are determined to avoid a return to the boom and bust economy of the past, which eroded the security many expected from their homes and created an uncertain climate for one of the most important long-term financial commitments which most people make.
>
> (DETR, 2000, p. 30)

This appeared to set government against direct intervention and favoured a cautious approach, which entailed setting the right parameters in which the market could operate.

However, as the discussion on the sub-prime mortgage crisis and Northern Rock showed, the benign economic conditions of steady but affordable growth did not last long. Even before 2007 there had been a feeling that there was a growing affordability problem in the UK. This was because of rapidly rising house price inflation, particularly in and around London and in the south of England, resulting from an increased demand for housing created by inward migration and changes to the labour market. This meant that the rather complacent view taken by government in 2000 could no longer be sustained, and a more direct form of intervention was sought.

Since 2003 there has been a succession of policies and reports aimed at dealing with the increasing problem of unaffordability. However, before looking at these, we need to mention one of the key paradoxes that affect housing both in the UK and elsewhere. On the one hand, households have become accustomed to their dwelling becoming a store of wealth that gives them and their children security. Therefore, for these households, appreciating house prices are seen as a benefit in that this heightens their sense of security. But, on the other hand, rising house prices make it harder for first time buyers to gain access to the market, without overstretching their resources and leaving themselves vulnerable to changes in interest rates. We could therefore argue that what best suits these households is a fall in house prices or, at worst, for them to remain static. However, once they become owner occupiers their interests change and falling house prices are the last thing they would wish for. So there is a paradox, in that rising housing prices make some of us feel more affluent and secure, whilst excluding others who are not yet on the housing ladder. Of course, this a very difficult conundrum for government to deal with: it needs to ensure that the 'feel good' factor remains, but also that first time buyers have a ready and sustainable means of meeting their legitimate aspirations.

One attempt to deal with this problem in England was the *Sustainable Communities Plan* (ODPM, 2003). This plan is concerned with developing four growth areas of new housing development in the south of England and to the north of London, where the demand for housing and house prices are high, but also to allow for the regeneration of abandoned and low-demand housing areas, involving mass demolition, in areas of the north and the Midlands. This latter policy has come to be called *housing market renewal*. The common theme of these two approaches of growth and renewal is the idea of 'building communities', be it from scratch or by reinvigorating depressed areas. The result is that the bulk of new housing investment is being targeted at these areas, with the effect that inclusion in a growth area or a housing market renewal pathfinder[2] has considerable consequences for local housing organisations. Moreover, the shift to large-scale and volume development favours large regional or national housing associations and has led to a rush by associations to join housing consortia or to merge to form a larger body capable of competing successfully for volume building.

An equally significant event was the publication in 2004 of the results of the Barker review on housing supply (HM Treasury, 2004). This looked at the need for new housing and suggested that the supply of both social and private housing should be increased considerably. The resulting report had a considerable impact on both subsequent policy and on the debate about the future of housing provision. Not only did it call for a considerable increase in expenditure on housing, it also opened up the debate on affordability and how this could be dealt with in a manner that was politically acceptable and achievable. The key problem was that much of the housing that was needed was in areas of existing high density, which would put a strain on the economic and environmental infrastructure of these areas. So the debate on housing supply expanded to include issues like school places, adequate water supplies, transport links and the future of the green belt.

In 2005 the government in England announced a policy that appeared to demonstrate a shift in attitude towards social housing (King, 2006). The Homes for All policy (ODPM, 2005), which was essentially a development of the Sustainable Communities Plan, involved the introduction of a First Time Buyer Initiative which allows 15,000 low income households and key workers to buy an equity share in a dwelling (many of these new dwellings will be built on publicly owned land). The most high profile part of the policy was the announcement of a competition for developers to provide what became known as the '£60,000 house', again using public land. It quickly became clear, however, that the price referred to the cost of building and not the price to the buyer. Of more actual significance, however, was the introduction of an initiative called Homebuy for social housing tenants to enable them to buy, at a discount, an equity share in their dwelling of between 50 and 100 per cent. The government suggested that this would make owning a dwelling affordable to around 300,000 tenants. The Homebuy initiative has been slow to take off, with the result that government has continued to tinker with the concept. In early 2007 the government proposed equity shares as low as 10 per cent and in 2008 it was proposed that the scheme be opened up to all first time buyers with an income below £60,000 per annum.

Of course, there is nothing new in the preparedness of government to use social housing to further owner occupation, as we have seen in our discussion of the Right to Buy. What is different with the Homes for All agenda, however, is that the proclaimed justification – owner occupation for all – was not so much that of independence or even choice, but social justice. The government's argument was that low income households deserved access to owner occupation just like the more affluent who already had ready access. This attempt to extend owner occupation was also seen in the establishment of the Hills review, which reported in 2007 (Hills, 2007) and looked at the future of low cost home ownership, as well as providing a justification for the continued need for social housing. As we saw in chapter 4, Hills argued strongly for the latter, but it might be seen as significant that government seems to have placed a higher priority on ownership than on renting, and that pursuing this agenda is now the main influence on social housing policy.

The last document we need to discuss may well be the most significant, at least as far as the future of housing in England is concerned. The 2007 Green Paper entitled *Homes for the Future: More Sustainable, More Affordable* (CLG, 2007) is important for the manner in which it seems explicitly to see social housing as a safety net. The Green Paper states that social housing exists 'to provide affordable homes to rent with security of tenure for families on low incomes, for people with severe disabilities, for frail older people and for other people for whom home ownership is unlikely to be the right option' (CLG, 2007, p. 72). Social housing is therefore housing of last resort for those who cannot enter the owner occupied market.

Whilst increases in the supply of social housing are envisaged, the Green Paper therefore put a much greater emphasis on increasing housing supply in owner occupied sectors. This, to an extent, builds on the policies in place since 2003 aimed at meeting housing demand and dealing with affordability in the south (ODPM, 2003) and extending owner occupation for those who are on low incomes or seen as key workers (ODPM, 2005). However, it is more explicit in that it lays down specific targets for dealing with the shortfall in housing supply. The 2007 Green Paper states that an extra 3 million dwellings should be provided by 2020 and that social housing building should increase from the level of 28,000 in 2006/07 to 50,000 per annum in 2010/11: were this maintained for the ensuing decade it would equate to 500,000 or 16.7 per cent of the total planned increase in dwellings by 2020.

However, this statement of intent was knocked off course almost immediately by the downturn in the housing market. With the number of housing transactions falling, mortgage rates increasing and first time buyers struggling to obtain finance, it is unlikely that these targets can be met. Government is persisting with them largely, one thinks, because they are so long term – to be achieved by 2020 – that it can hope that the market will turn and so it can make up any shortfall. However, a target date of 2020, 13 years from the start of the policy, and with two or even three general elections in that period, was always likely to be a statement of intent rather than a definite commitment with funding attached.

But whether achievable or not, this policy statement, along with the other recent reports, plans and policies, shows that government cannot resist intervening in housing markets. Owner occupation is too important and significant a tenure to be left to the vagaries of markets, and so government must intervene. It is accepted that a government's popularity is tied to the state of the housing market – both the Conservative government in 1992–3 and the Labour government in 2007–8 took a nosedive in popularity when the housing market headed downwards – and so maintaining the market is seen as essential. But, of course, its interventions, such as the Right to Buy and MITR, have an impact on the market in themselves (why else introduce them!).

But the downturn in UK and US housing markets in 2007 and 2008 shows that whilst government might intervene, it cannot control them. Indeed, we might argue that the actions of the UK government in 2008 to nationalise several banks rather demonstrates that *markets can control governments*. The interconnected global nature of markets means that a national government, even one as large as that of the UK, is impotent rather than in control of affairs. It has to react and try to influence rather than direct what is happening in the market. This means that it is somewhat at the mercy of a market that it cannot afford to ignore, but which it cannot fully understand or control. Of course, this means that, even though interventions may fail, no government can refuse to undertake them.

Controlling rents: an example of unintended consequences

If owner occupation dominated housing markets at the end of the twentieth century, the situation at the start of the century was very different. In the UK the private rented sector was once the largest housing sector, comprising 89 per cent of households in 1915. The figure has now declined to 12 per cent, although this represents something of a fight back from the low of 9.7 per cent in 2001 (Wilcox, 2008). The decline of private renting is a key example of unintended consequences in housing, in which a well-intentioned policy has had the effect of constraining the tenure and preventing it from providing housing in either sufficient quantity or quality.

Two reasons are commonly given for the decline of private renting. One is the provision of large-scale subsidies to alternative forms of provision, particularly social housing, but also tax relief for owner occupiers. Private renting has not had the same level of financial support. Indeed the reverse is the case, and this brings us to the second reason. Many governments have imposed rent controls on the private rented sector, which means that the landlord may not increase rents above a certain ceiling set by government. This makes rents more affordable and thus within the reach of more households, but it also has the effect of reducing the ability of landlords to make a reasonable return on their investments and so they have tended to leave the sector. We shall therefore explore rent control policies as a form of government intervention, which has certainly influenced housing markets, but perhaps not in the manner intended. We shall relate this discussion to the nature of markets considered in chapter 3 and back this up with some examples.

Rent controls were introduced in the UK in 1915 as an emergency measure. The purpose for this was to deal with social unrest caused by accusations of profiteering on the part of landlords. The outbreak of war in

1914 had increased the demand for rented housing, yet prevented an increase in supply. More workers were needed for war manufacturing; resources were needed for the war effort and could not be spared for housebuilding. The result was an increase in rents in many urban areas. This was seen as profiteering by many tenants and led to rent strikes across the country, but particularly in Glasgow in 1915. The government responded to this with the *Increase of Rent and Mortgage Interest (War Restrictions) Act 1915*, which imposed a ceiling on rents and mortgage interest at their August 1914 levels. As the name of the measure suggests, this was intended to be temporary and only for the duration of the war, but in fact statutory rent controls continued to exist in some form between 1915 and 1957, and again from 1965 and 1989. This shows that rent controls are difficult to remove once they have been imposed because their removal, and a consequent return to market rents, would be seen to cause considerable hardship for tenants.

However, the effect of rent control was to reduce drastically the incentive to supply, because landlords were not able to adjust their rents in line with changes in their expenditure. However, it also had the effect of increasing demand because dwellings were let at cheaper rents than would be set in a free market and so were more affordable. This problem of excess demand would ordinarily have been met by an increase in rents, which in turn would have acted as a signal to increase supply. But rent controls not only prevented these market signals from operating, they actually created the opposite effect. Rents could not rise, which was of benefit to existing tenants, but landlords had a reduced incentive to invest in their properties because they could not secure a reasonable return. There was therefore a reduction in the quality of dwellings as repairs and improvements were postponed. In addition, many landlords left the sector, often by selling to the sitting tenant. The effects of rent control are summarised in Table 5.2.

The main problem of rent control was that, unlike later forms of subsidy offered to owner occupiers and social landlords, it directly benefited tenants

Table 5.2   The effects of rent control

- Cheaper rents that are affordable to a greater number of households.
- This leads to an increase in demand.
- But also to reduced supply because landlords leave the sector as their income is reduced and they cannot gain a reasonable return on their investment.
- Those landlords who remain are less likely to maintain their properties, leading to a decline in quality.
- Illegal and informal markets are created, and tenants are harassed, to circumvent rent restrictions.

at the expense of the landlord. As Albon and Stafford (1987) state, 'Rental market controls are a clear violation of individual rights' (p. vii). They impinge on the owner's property rights and limit his or her right to use and transfer their property.

Rent control, therefore, is a form of regulation that forces one party to a contract to make a contribution to the other, but without being compensated by government for doing so. Unlike subsidies to social landlords, the government did not provide the subsidy but rather forced landlords to subsidise tenants by debarring them from increasing their rents. The consequence of this form of subsidy was to present landlords with a huge disincentive to invest or even stay in the market. The policy, however, is cost-free to government.

In addition to this Albon and Stafford (1987) see the imposition of rent controls as having perverse consequences. They state that controls lead to:

> an excess demand for housing which fosters unfortunate practices such as discrimination on various grounds other than willingness and ability to pay rent, and the creation of a black market. Further, rent and eviction controls have a major impact on the mobility of labour.
>
> (Albon and Stafford, 1987, p. v)

If a household has a rent controlled dwelling they may be reluctant to give it up, at least not without a considerable increase in their income to compensate for the higher rent.

But Albon and Stafford also suggest that rent controls might not actually help those intended but instead be rather arbitrary in their effects. Whilst rent controls have obvious implications for income distribution, this does not necessarily benefit those on low incomes, but instead the effect is random 'without regards to the financial circumstances of either [landlord or tenant]. If the state really believes that tenants should be subsidised, it should ask if it should be the landlord or the state who should be responsible for this subsidy' (p. 22).

Sowell (2007) discusses the effects of rent controls, but concentrates on the USA. He shows that where rent controls apply on a blanket basis, as in New York, 'even luxurious housing becomes low-rent housing' (p. 47). The effect of controls is that large apartments, lived in by relatively affluent households, may be much cheaper than smaller apartments that are exempt from control. This means that in places like New York the wealthy benefit from rent controls as much as, if not more than, the poor. Sowell, therefore, concurs with Albon and Stafford on the fact that who benefits and who loses from rent control is arbitrary, dependent on who has the good luck to be inside and the bad luck to be outside. He states that in 2001 a quarter of households in rent controlled accommodation in San Francisco had incomes in excess of $100,000 per annum.

But, according to Sowell, the problem with rent control is more general. He states that during World War II low rents caused by rent control allowed young people to move away from their parents earlier, and for other families to afford larger accommodation than would otherwise have been possible. But this created a shortage of rented housing, 'even though there was not any greater physical scarcity of housing relative to the total population' (p. 40). Once rent controls ended after the war, these shortages disappeared. He states that 'As rents rose in a free market, some childless couples living in four-bedroom apartments decided that they would live in two-bedroom apartments and save the difference in the rent' (p. 41). Also young people stayed at home with parents for longer. But, as a result of this change in behaviour, families could now find affordable apartments.

Sowell states that rent controls reduce the incentives for individuals to limit their own use of those scarce resources desired by others. Therefore rent controls can lead to under occupation. He states that in 2001 49 per cent of San Francisco's rent controlled apartments were occupied by a one-person household, whilst the figure for Manhattan was 48 per cent. Similarly, the elderly have little incentive to vacate rent controlled apartments that they would normally vacate. Sowell states that 'rent control reduces the rate of housing turnover' (p. 42).

It can be argued that rent controls affect the supply of housing just as they do demand. Sowell states that 'Nine years after the end of World War II, not a single new building had been built in Melbourne, Australia, because of rent control laws there which made buildings unprofitable' (2007, p. 43). Likewise, rent control laws introduced in Santa Monica, California, in 1979 saw building permits decline to a tenth of their 1974 level. The reason for this is that investors could not see themselves making a reasonable return on their investment.

But Sowell argues that it is not only the supply of new dwellings that declines, but also the supply of existing dwellings, which landlords neglect to maintain and repair 'since the housing shortage makes it unnecessary for them to maintain the appearance of their premises in order to attract tenants. Thus housing tends to deteriorate faster under rent control and to have fewer replacements when it wears out' (p. 43).

Landlords also do not have to respond to the normal signals, particularly with regard to competition: 'Shortages mean that the seller no longer has to please the buyer. This is why landlords can let maintenance and other services deteriorate under rent control' (Sowell, 2007, p. 51). Because there is a tendency for excess demand in rent controlled housing markets, landlords do not need to be aware of their competitors but can effectively tell prospective tenants to take it or leave it.

Somewhat perversely, however, the only profitable form of renting is luxury accommodation. This is because this type of rented housing is often exempt from controls. Accordingly, Sowell argues that 'a policy intended to make housing affordable for the poor has had the net effect of shifting resources toward the building of housing that is affordable only by the affluent and rich, since luxury housing is often exempt from rent control' (2007, p. 44).

Albon and Stafford offer a summary of what is wrong with the policy:

> Rent controls provide relief for sitting tenants, but prospective tenants and those tenants wishing to move can be very adversely affected in the long run. Landlords denied an economic return will sell as soon as an opportunity presents itself and invest elsewhere. Frequently, however, the landlord is locked in and under-maintains his property leading to premature decay and clearance. Low rents encourage the overconsumption of house room since there is no incentive to economise. Finally, all tenants, and also landlords, rich and poor, are treated alike.
>
> (Albon and Stafford, 1987, pp. 24–5)

This is a rather damning indictment of a policy aimed at helping those on low incomes and making housing more affordable. Yet, despite these problems, rent controls were maintained in the UK for most of the twentieth century. Several attempts in the 1930s and 1950s were made to abolish rent controls, but world wars and politics intervened to thwart such attempts, which were made mainly by Conservative governments.

When rent controls were abolished in 1989, there had been three significant changes to the private rented sector. First, the sector was now much smaller. In the late 1950s nearly half of Britain's households were in private rented housing, whereas in 1989 the figure was only around 10 per cent. This meant that the tenure had become much less significant politically and in electoral terms and so could be more readily ignored. The priority was now owner occupation and the greatest political controversy was over the Conservative government's plans for the use of private finance in social housing (King, 1996). Second, the image of private landlords was such that they were not deemed especially deserving of support. The notion that landlords did not maintain their properties and would use coercion to gain possession had taken hold, even if it was not particularly typical of landlords' behaviour.

But third and most significantly, by 1989 there was a comprehensive Housing Benefit system supporting the private rented sector. Low income private tenants could now receive their full rent in benefit. This had the effect of cushioning rent increases, which allowed landlords to increase rents without this having a dramatic impact on tenants. As a result it was hoped that private renting would become more profitable again. Indeed, government certainly intended rents to rise as a means of encouraging increased supply.

However, we can argue that it was not the operation of free markets that allowed landlords to raise rents; instead it was the operation of the Housing Benefit system, which paid the actual rent to eligible claimants, that allowed landlords to increase rents. As a result average rents for the sector rose from £24.00 per week in 1988 to £72.01 for a market rent in 1998: a 300 per cent increase in only a decade (Wilcox, 2005). This might have meant that the sector was more profitable and there was indeed a modest increase in the sector. But the government did not allow the market to develop freely and this was largely because of the way in which the private rented sector now interacted with the Housing Benefit system.

Decontrolling rents: another example of unintended consequences

The problem was that both landlords and tenants were insulated from the effect of rent increases by Housing Benefit, but government had to pick up the bill instead. If landlords raised the rents, this increase was not borne by many tenants but by Housing Benefit. Indeed landlords now had a definite incentive to choose Housing Benefit claimants as tenants precisely because rent payment was not a problem. This was further compounded by the fact that the benefit could be paid direct to the landlord.

But this was a situation that central government did not consider sustainable. Rent controls were a policy measure which did not directly affect government expenditure, in that landlords paid the cost of the subsidy. Yet the comprehensive nature of the Housing Benefit system had meant that the abolition of controls considerably increased government expenditure. As we have seen, rents rose by 300 per cent between 1988 and 1998. Throughout the 1980s Housing Benefit grew at the rate of 4 per cent a year, whereas in the first half of the 1990s this increased to 11 per cent per annum. These trends in expenditure have led government to alter the benefit system to limit the effects of rent increases. Housing Benefit has been restricted in all tenures, but it is only in the private rented sector that eligibility has been reduced.

In January 1996 the local reference rents system was introduced. The local reference rent is the average rent for a particular property type in a particular area. The purpose of this change was to try and halt the increase in rents, or even to decrease them, by altering the incentives that operated in the

Housing Benefit system. Instead of private sector tenants receiving the full rent charged by the landlord, they would now receive payments up to a maximum determined by what was considered to be the appropriate level for the household and the local reference rent. This meant that the size and composition of the household was taken into account to ensure that households were not underoccupying dwellings, but living in properties appropriate to their needs. This was an attempt to deal with so-called 'upmarketing', whereby households would move to larger accommodation funded through the open-ended Housing Benefit system. Therefore the Housing Benefit system, at least insofar as the private sector is concerned, was no longer open-ended. Since 1996 benefit has not necessarily been paid to cover the actual rent in the private rented sector. However, social tenants can still receive the full amount.

A further change limiting Housing Benefit payments for single persons under 25 was introduced in October 1996. The so-called 'single room rent' measure limited benefit to the amount equivalent to the rent charged for shared accommodation. This meant that tenants under 25 would have to move to shared accommodation or fund the difference themselves. As with the local reference rent system, this rule only applied in the private rented sector.

The effect of these changes was to reverse the increase in market activity. Wilcox (1999) showed the effect of these restrictions was a reduction of 100,000 private tenants claiming Housing Benefit between May 1997 and May 1998 'and most of that fall can be attributed to the benefit restrictions' (p. 72). In 1996, 46.6 per cent of private tenants were in receipt of Housing Benefit compared to only 28.7 per cent in 2003 (Wilcox, 2008). It appears that private landlords have become less willing to let to those on Housing Benefit, reversing the trend of the early 1990s.

What this discussion shows is that government feels it cannot let rents find their own levels. This is not because it is particularly antagonistic towards markets, but rather because it could not decouple one part of the housing system from another. The Housing Benefit system was now so thoroughly integrated into the private rented market that any changes in rents would have considerable consequences for government spending. It obviously could not readily abolish Housing Benefit, so instead it sought ways to moderate the consequences of its market rent policy by limiting the eligibility that private rented tenants have to the benefit. We can see this as a form of *administrative rent control*, where government uses one system – Housing Benefit – to manage another one – private sector rents.

This discussion also shows that, whilst government might seek to remedy one problem in a market, it might inadvertently create another which it considers equally serious. In this case government tried to liberate a market, but the consequence of this was to increase its commitment to pay benefit. However, in dealing with this latter situation, government has now created disincentives for landlords to house the poorest households.

The change in rent regulation in the private sector also demonstrates the long-term nature of housing issues. This is not because government has thought ahead, although politicians will always claim that is what they do, but because of the complexity of housing systems, which are open to external influence and which seek to integrate the decisions of millions of individuals. These decisions interrelate in an unpredictable and non-patterned manner, but their consequences are all too real. Once a situation has developed, like the decline of private rental markets, it cannot be easily remedied. And even if government can come up with a viable plan, there is every likelihood that its new policy will interact with existing policies in a manner that cannot be predicted, and that new vested interests and incentives will be created. Government will then have to respond to these changes, and so it goes on. A further example of this constant churning in the face of complexity is that of housing allowances. We have already touched on the manner in which Housing Benefit in the UK relates to the private rented sector, but we need to investigate the issue of housing allowances in more detail.

Think point

Is a free market in rented housing possible? Is it desirable?

Housing allowances: the creation of incentives

As we saw in chapter 4, the balance of government subsidies has shifted away from object subsides and towards subject subsidies. This has occurred in many developed countries (Kemp, 1997, 2007b), where the emphasis has shifted from the quantity of housing that is needed to the quality of what exists and whether low income households can gain access to it.

What is interesting is that whilst some countries, like Australia and New Zealand, have shifted towards an almost exclusive reliance on subject subsidies, other countries, like the UK, have a hybrid system that mixes object and subject subsidies together. The result is that households can receive a housing allowance, which allows them to pay the rent on a subsidised social dwelling. It is the manner in which the two forms of subsidy interact and alter the behaviour of both landlords and tenants that is particularly important in countries such as the UK.[3]

Housing allowances exist to help low income households pay their housing costs. In some countries this can include mortgage interest, but it is more common that housing allowance systems are reserved for assisting people on low income to pay their rent (Kemp, 2007b). For instance, the Housing Benefit system in the UK excludes owner occupiers from the scheme. However, tenants in all the rented sectors are eligible, although different rules apply which either affect the claimant or the organisation that receives the benefit. The key determinants are the income of the claimant and the type of landlord.

The UK system is unique in that, in some circumstances, once eligibility is established the claimant is entitled to payment of all of their rent. Thus higher rents mean higher Housing Benefit payments. Since 1996 this situation has only applied in the social sector. As we saw when discussing the private rented sector above, there are restrictions on the amount of benefit that will be paid in this sector. The local reference rent mechanism limited benefit payments to a reasonable rent according to the type of property that the household would reasonably be expected to reside in. The single room rent regulation limited the amount that single people under 25 can receive.

In other countries the amount of housing allowance payable is restricted to a fixed percentage, with the tenants having to fund the difference from their other income. The reason for this situation is to ensure that claimants remain aware of rent levels and of any changes that occur (Kemp, 2007b). In the UK, rents can increase without having any impact on the tenant and therefore changes in rent levels have no incentive effect. This is not the case where the claimant must contribute from their own income.

There is virtually a commonality of view that the system of Housing Benefit in the UK needs to be reformed. However, it has proven rather difficult to achieve a consensus on just what is the nature of the problem and therefore on what reforms are needed. Successive governments have been concerned by the increasing cost of Housing Benefit and, as we have seen, this was one of the reasons for the limits put in place in 1996. However, since 1996 costs have only remained stable but have not come down, and this is a cause for concern, especially as Britain experienced steady economic growth and relatively high levels of employment from 1993 until 2008. This implies that, if the UK were to face a recession, the costs of Housing Benefit could start to increase again.

But the problems go further than just the cost. The 2000 Housing Green Paper offered a comprehensive list of the system's problems, which included administrative complexity, propensity to fraud, a lack of understanding of entitlements, no link between rent levels and quality, deterrence of people

Table 5.3   The problems of means testing

Critics such as Field (1996) point to three key problems with means tested benefits:

- disincentives to work due to benefit withdrawal as income rises;
- the creation of social division between those who pay taxes and those who receive the benefit;
- incentive to worsen one's situation, or to lie about work, savings or relationships.

from taking jobs and the fact that Housing Benefit takes responsibility away from tenants as they have little interest in rent levels (DETR, 2000).

But there are two further – and related – problems with the Housing Benefit system not mentioned by the government in 2000. One of these problems is general to many housing allowance systems, whilst the other is more specific to the UK hybrid system. However, this second problem is again instructive in terms of the manner in which housing subsidies can create incentives, which are destructive of the particular system, but which are difficult to replace.

The first problem is one that we considered in chapter 4 when looking at subject subsidies. The Housing Benefit system operates on the basis of *means testing* (see Table 5.3). The amount of benefit reduces as income rises and thus the system favours the poorest. This allows government to target subsides on those most in need, but there are a number of problems with means testing. First, the severity of the tapers used to withdraw income may act as a disincentive to take up employment. Benefit is withdrawn quickly as income rises. The current taper is 65 per cent, which means that for every extra pound in income, 65 pence is taken from Housing Benefit. However, this problem becomes worse, in that as income rises, individuals pay more in tax and National Insurance. This means that some claimants, such as lone parents, can have an effective marginal tax rate of over 90 per cent (Kemp, 2007c). This is a key problem with housing allowance systems in that it creates considerable disincentives to work.

But there are further issues relating to means testing. It can be argued, for instance, that means testing creates a divided society (Field, 1996). This is because a majority of those who receive the benefit tend not to be paying taxes and therefore are not contributing to the cost of the benefit system. This means that taxpayers might not feel they are receiving anything back from their taxes and have little in common with benefit recipients.

Some critics, such as Field (1996) and Murray (1996), argue that means testing is actually immoral. As households receive more benefits when their income is lowest, they have strong incentives to lie about their income and not to take up employment. Means testing, according to Field, is a disincentive to save, to be honest and to try and be independent. Field argues that means tested benefits are prone to fraud and encourage an illegal informal economy.

Think point

Are there any viable alternatives to means testing?

The second and related issue is that of *dependency*. People can become dependent on benefit because of the steep rate of withdrawal of benefit as income rises. A claimant has to earn so much above the basic income support level before they are appreciably better off that they may find it easier to stay on benefit. As a result, the issue of economic dependency or worklessness has come to the fore. Wilcox (2008) shows that over half of all households in rented accommodation are in receipt of benefit, with the private rented sector the lowest at 28.3 per cent, local authorities at 62.65 per cent and housing associations at 67.1 per cent. In 2008 the housing minister in England announced that dealing with worklessness was to become a priority, with the possibility of social tenants being contractually committed to seeking employment under sanction of eviction.

But the problem is rather more complex than just tenants' dependency on Housing Benefit. In the UK the majority of benefit is not paid to the tenant but directly to their landlords. As Irvine *et al.* (2007) show, this is the case for all local authority claimants, while 92 per cent of those renting from housing associations and 60 per cent of private tenants have their rent paid directly to their landlord. The issue therefore is *who controls Housing Benefit*. In particular, do landlords have some control over the benefit because of their ability to increase rents (King, 2000, 2006)? In the social sector, where over 50 per cent of landlords' income derives from Housing Benefit, we might argue that they have an incentive to maximise the number of eligible claimants. Tenants on Housing Benefit therefore carry a premium that tenants in employment do not. The issue has become more important for social landlords as a result of the reduction of capital grants since 1989 and the increased reliance on private finance (King, 2006). As we shall see in chapter 6, Housing Benefit can be used to offset the risk of borrowing private finance. However, we should note that the problem with this form of subsidy capture was precisely why the previous government in 1996 introduced local reference rents. Most claimants, of course, might well be entirely happy with rent payments paid directly to their landlord, in that they have no personal responsibility for paying their rent and so rent levels remain a matter of indifference to them.

One of the key problems with this housing allowance system is that it can be controlled by landlords and the incentives make it attractive for them to maximise the number of claimants housed in order to offset the reduction in other subsidies. In 2002 the UK government came up with a means of dealing with this. However, it has been markedly reluctant to introduce the new system in all tenures.

Interestingly the proposed reforms came in a document entitled *Building Choice and Responsibility: A Radical Agenda for Housing Benefit* (DWP, 2002). This links directly with the issues we discussed in chapter 2, and shows how subsidies can be connected to these important concepts. In terms of concrete proposals, what it shows is that government, in the UK at least, is aware of the incentive effects of particular types of subsidy.

Currently, the system only applies to the private rented sector, having been introduced in eighteen so-called 'pathfinder' areas in 2003–4, initially to evaluate the scheme, and only extended to all new claimants across the UK from April 2008. The new system involves two important changes, which could be implemented independently of each other.

First, instead of a claim being assessed on the actual rent, a flat rate standard local housing allowance will be applied. This means that if a claimant can find cheaper accommodation than the standard allowance, they can keep the difference. Alternatively, they can top up the rent if they choose a more expensive property. Thus the system includes what has been termed *shopping incentives*, in that it encourages households to make choices within their income constraints (Kemp, 2007c). The allowance is increased for large families to allow them to live in larger dwellings.

Second, payments of benefit, except in exceptional cases of vulnerability and when there is more than eight weeks' arrears, will be made to the tenants and not the landlord. As we have seen above, the overwhelming majority of claimants do not receive any payments, but rather it goes directly to their landlord. This is administratively simpler for both landlord and benefits administration, but means that tenants have no responsibility for rent payments. This has now changed and tenants must make arrangements to pay over their benefit. The fear is that many tenants, being on very low incomes, will use their benefit to fund other activities and so arrears levels and evictions will increase.

However, the reforms are not as radical as they might have been, in that the current income tests still apply, as does the 65 per cent taper rate and the single room rent regulation. It is therefore questionable how far the issue of the poverty trap has really been addressed in these reforms.

Kemp (2007c), in summarising the early evaluation of the pathfinder areas, has stated that there has been relatively little disruption, with no huge increase in arrears or evictions. In particular, he stated that there has not been any major change in rent levels. However, it needs to be remembered that the number of benefit recipients in the private rented sector had already declined as a result of the 1996 restrictions and most private landlords do not now let to benefit claimants. The allocation practices of private landlords are only restricted by the market they operate in, and so if they have alternatives to Housing Benefit claimants, they are perfectly at liberty to discriminate.

Where the reforms would have a much greater effect is in the social sector, particularly in the ending of payment direct to landlords. This is because, unlike private landlords, social landlords are unable to alter their allocations policies to suit their financial priorities. Also, as we have argued, many social landlords have become dependent on Housing Benefit as a secure and risk-free source of income. However, despite apparently remaining committed to introducing local housing allowances in the social sector, the government has backed off from actually going ahead. This has been justified on the grounds that many other changes are under way in the social sector, several of which we shall discuss in chapter 6. Some of these are of a technical nature and would make it hard for a local housing allowance to work (see the discussion on rent restructuring in chapter 6), but for the most part it is a case of prioritising which reforms are most significant (or less controversial) from the government's perspective.

Of course, it is currently too early to tell what impact these changes will have. But we can see that they are limited and will only tackle part of the problems relating to Housing Benefit. In particular, the issue of economic dependency has not yet been fully addressed.

More generally, this discussion has shown that government intervention through the provision of subject subsidies has created a series of incentives for both landlords and tenants which have skewed market provision. It shows that government cannot intervene in a market in a neutral manner and that, however it acts, it will create unplanned opportunities for some groups and unwanted threats to others, which might then have to be dealt with later by another form of intervention.

But what government cannot do is *not* try to influence markets. If there is a significant number of households with low, or even no, income, government must find some means of assisting them. This might be direct provision but, as we have seen, this is currently not the chosen option. But even if government did build houses, unless it offered them rent-free, there would still be the need for some form of assistance with income.

Think point

What is the biggest priority: encouraging low income households to take more responsibility for their housing, or securing the financial viability of landlords?

Conclusions

In this chapter we have explored the main ways in which governments seek to influence housing markets without directly providing housing itself. This is through personal subsidies to owner occupiers and renters, and through the regulation of private sector rents. We have seen that the intervention is extensive and has existed for nearly a century.

But we have also seen that there are almost certain to be unintended consequences arising from government intervention. This may lead to the virtual collapse of what was once the majority tenure in a country or, less dramatically, it might encourage landlords to favour or exclude particular types of tenant.

The existence of unintended consequences, assuming that they are inevitable, means two things. First, that government intervention may well go wrong or results in effects that were not expressly anticipated; and second, that it makes government intervention inevitable, in that it generates future problems that will need to be solved. Failure of government action, therefore, does not lead politicians to suggest that they should not intervene, rather that they should intervene *more effectively* to try and get things right *this time*. Over time what this means is that they seek to control rather than just influence. But whilst governments cannot control markets – even though they may seek to – they might be more successful with a form of provision that they themselves have created, and this is the issue that chapter 6 seeks to explore.

Further reading

A lot of the really interesting and meaty books on owner occupation are now quite old and have dated somewhat. However, this is more than made up for by the seriousness of this literature. It was also a period when the debate in the UK and elsewhere about owner occupation and the Right to Buy was at its peak. One example is Ball (1983), who takes an explicitly political economy approach, albeit of the Marxist variety. Forrest *et al.* (1990) offer an interesting view that considers the UK from a comparative perspective. A completely different (liberal) view, but one that contains a very comprehensive review of the debates on the tenure, can be found in Saunders (1990).

On rent control, readers should turn to Albon and Stafford (1987) which, whilst using some economic analysis, is generally readable and clear, if rather polemical at times. The best source for a discussion on housing allowances from a comparative perspective is Kemp (2007a). Finally, my book *Choice and the End of Social Housing* (2006) provides an overview of government intervention in housing and its effects on some of the mechanisms considered in this chapter.

6

Controlling housing

Learning outcomes

- The changing nature of public provision.
- The accountability of social housing.
- Controlling social provision using market disciplines.
- How government maintains control without direct ownership.
- The effects of government control on housing providers.

Introduction

Local authorities in the UK built over six million dwellings in the twentieth century, and for part of that century a majority of Scots lived in council housing. This housing, it was understood, was for local people. It may not have been for the poorest – there was no comprehensive system of housing allowances until 1972 – but it most certainly was for people who could claim a local connection. Typically, the housing was allocated on the basis of length of time on the waiting list, and a household could only get a place on that list if they were local.

But then local authorities were run by elected officials and so could claim to be locally accountable. Part of the cost of that housing was paid for by local rate payers. And, of course, housing being an immobile asset, the housing itself was physically located in the local area. So, we might say, council housing was built locally, managed locally and for local people.

Yet, if we fast-forward to the twenty-first century, we see a totally different situation. We now, of course, talk of social housing instead of council housing, because many of the dwellings are owned by housing associations.

In fact a significant amount of what used to be council housing has been transferred to housing associations so that the local authority no longer owns any housing at all. But what is particularly important is that central government now controls what happens with regard to social housing, not locally elected councils. Social housing, the government insists, is a national asset.

But, of course, the housing is still in the same place, and people still want housing in the areas that they know, where they were brought up, have family and friends and where they have jobs. So social housing is still an important local resource. However, it is now controlled much more by central government.

There are a number of reasons we can point to for this situation (which are summarised in Table 6.1). First, whilst local authorities did use local income, and rents of course, to fund council housebuilding, they also relied on government subsidies. In addition, as we saw in chapter 5, many social tenants rely on Housing Benefit, which is largely funded centrally. We have seen that successive governments have been concerned with the costs of the benefit system (see chapter 5) and have sought to reduce the capital cost of housebuilding as a means of reducing public expenditure (see chapter 4). Government, therefore, seeks to control social housing to limit its current and future expenditure. What makes it able to do this, to an extent at least, is that social housing generates an income through rents, and so government can force social landlords to increase rents to offset a reduction in subsidies.

Second, social housing does not win many votes at the national level, at least not in comparison to universal forms of provision, like health care, or larger tenures, like owner occupation. Indeed the particularist nature of social housing is of great importance here. Social housing is means tested and provided for a selected group, and this means it tends to garner less support than services provided for all or for a majority. Social housing can be seen

Table 6.1 Why government tries to control local housing provision

---

- The need to control subsidy contributions to housebuilding and housing allowances.

- Social housing is politically unpopular due to its particularist nature.

- Housebuilding is expensive and debt liabilities are long term.

- Local authorities are a rival source of electoral legitimacy and might oppose central government policies.

- Past failures to control lead central government to try harder.

---

as a potential liability for government and so needs to be controlled. Where government does seek to alter and reform it – and these are very much top-down changes – it seeks to transform social housing such that it mirrors the purported virtues of owner occupation. Hence, as we shall see in this chapter, government has emphasised choice and efficiency as key elements for reform.

Third, building houses is expensive and, once they are built, they last for many years. Indeed, social landlords are often paying off debts incurred in development for decades. This means that the financial consequences of social housing are considerable. Hence governments keen to control public expenditure will bear down on the activities of social landlords to ensure they meet government priorities.

Fourth, the fact that local authorities are elected bodies means there might be political conflict between the centre and locality. Indeed, in the UK over the last 30 years we have had two relatively long periods of single party government – the Conservatives from 1979 to 1997 and Labour from 1997 onwards – with the consequence that local government tends to be increasingly dominated by opposition parties elected in protest against central government policies. Whilst it might be healthy for a democracy to have a plurality of political control, it does not help central government to implement its policies. What has tended to happen, therefore, is that central government has accreted more power in order to control local authorities and thus ensure they fulfil policies in the manner central government requires.

The final point is linked to this. Even though government seeks to control local institutions, it often fails to do so. This is partly due to conflicting control, but it is also due to complexity and a lack of understanding of issues at the local level. However, the response to failure has not been to increase local autonomy, but instead to increase the level of direct control.

One means by which this control has been achieved appears at first to be perverse and possibly even counterproductive. Government has effectively privatised social housing by preventing local authorities from building and placing that responsibility on housing associations. It has used a policy of stock transfer, whereby council housing is sold to a new or existing association. As a result, housing associations will soon make up the majority of social landlords (Wilcox, 2008). But, this privatisation is only *apparently* perverse: in practice it has assisted central government in controlling social housing, and we shall spend much of the first part of this chapter seeking to understand why this is so.

So we will look at how government has sought to use financial mechanisms to control the activities of social landlords. We have seen that they can only influence markets, and this is often difficult both to achieve and predict the outcome. But with social housing central government can exercise much more direct control. This is because it provides much of the finance and because many of the structures have been established through legislation, and what government makes it can also break.

The majority of the discussion in this chapter relates to social housing in the UK or rather, for the most part, only to England. This inevitably limits the discussion, but I do believe that there is much that we can generalise from in this discussion. This is because other countries also have social housing and, as we saw in chapter 4, whether we define it by who it's for, who owns it or who pays for it, central government is inevitably involved. In other countries social landlords have more freedom, but this is a question of degree rather than an absolute situation. However, it is also fair to say that many, if not most, academics and commentators see direct provision of housing as the preferred option in terms of government action. We saw in chapter 4 that Hills (2007) argues that there are advantages in social provision, such as increased quality, greater affordability, and avoiding discrimination and social polarisation. Hills's view is one that is widely shared as a justification for continued government support for social housing. Therefore, we can extrapolate some more general points from this parochial discussion on social housing in England.

In this chapter, then, we shall consider how central government controls social housing and the consequences that arise from this. We shall begin with a brief look at how social housing can be made accountable and then examine the particular mechanisms of control. This leads on to a discussion of the use of private finance and the role of housing associations and how this does not diminish the control central government can exercise. In the final part of the chapter we shall look at some of the consequences of this form of intervention, particularly at the notions of risk and commercialisation.

The accountability of social housing

As we mentioned at the start of this chapter, the majority of social housing in the UK has been built by locally elected authorities. We can therefore state that it has been provided locally for local people, by local people and it should therefore be accountable to them. If the local populace do not like how their council is managing the housing stock, they can vote them out and replace them with others committed to the majority view.

Yet this might not work in practice. There might not be a majority view, only lots of competing minority views. In any case, getting rid of a majority on the local council might not be easy and may take several years, if it is possible at all. In addition, whilst social housing is expensive to build and the way it is allocated might be controversial, most local people will not be eligible for a particularist service based on need and vulnerability. So, if we cannot be housed in it, why should we bother how it is run? This might mean that managers are therefore able to exercise a large amount of control over how services are run. But, in any case, we should expect this, as local managers not only have control over resources, but will have a level of knowledge and skills that will outweigh those of the vast majority of local electors.

But central government has also provided much of the resources to build and manage social housing. It therefore requires some say in how local housing services are provided and run, so it can justify its expenditure to taxpayers and ensure any money is well spent. Thus social landlords have to be accountable to central government, as well as the local electorate.

But in our discussion on subject subsidies we pointed to the possibility of producer capture, whereby the producers of a service are able to control the provision and so allow their interests to dominate. Boyne *et al.* (2003) argued that there were three possible reasons for this capture of public services. First, many were monopolies or exerted considerable dominance over the provision of services. This is the case with social housing, in that most landlords in an area will tend to co-operate rather than compete with each other. In any case the local authority – or the housing association it has transferred its stock to – will often be by far the largest local provider. Monopolies do not have to have such regard for the needs of consumers, who are unable to go elsewhere for the service. Second, public services tend not to have valid indicators of performance. They do not make a profit or a loss and they are not competing for market share. So, again, they are not being tested in terms of their level of service. Third, because public bodies are often so large, they face problems in co-ordination and diseconomies of scale. This might be less of an issue with local social landlords but some municipal authorities are very large with a number nearing the 100,000 dwelling mark. This size of organisation is difficult to control and it is difficult to give the impression that each tenant or applicant matters. In addition, some of the largest housing associations are now national bodies and this might cause co-ordination problems between the central administration and local offices and agencies. As a result of these problems the issue of the accountability of social landlords has become increasingly important, with landlords having to justify their role and show that they are efficient and effective in their service delivery. So how do we measure whether social housing is doing what it should be doing?

The first issue is to decide just who is best able to answer this question. Is it society itself? Is it the government, which is deemed to be acting on society's behalf? Or should it be Parliament, which is meant to hold government to account? But should we not take into account the voice of the users, who are the ones with the day-to-day experience? Put more simply, should social housing be accountable to government or to the users?

The obvious way in which social landlords are held accountable is through the preparation and public presentation of financial accounts. This is where they record income and expenditure, and assets and liabilities for a given period. These will be audited independently and presented for public scrutiny. In order to achieve this, an organisation will undertake continuous recording of financial transactions. Accounts can be used to prove that income has been used properly, and that money has not been wasted or used frivolously.

Yet we need to remember that all this information is historical: the money will already be spent by the time we see the accounts. Therefore in addition to accounts an organisation will need to have financial regulations. These are a set of rules and policies that determine ways in which money can be spent, and which will often be backed up by a system of internal audit to ensure the rules are followed.

But there are other ways in which housing organisations can be made accountable. In the case of local authorities, this is through the election of councillors who are then periodically held accountable to the local electorate. Another way of ensuring accountability is through holding important meetings in public so that local people can see how decisions are taken and how their representatives behave. In the case of housing association boards of management they can be made to represent their local communities in terms of ethnic diversity and can include tenant representatives. Likewise, social landlords can seek to ensure that their staff is representative of their communities in terms of gender and ethnicity. Finally, housing organisations may have to show that they are following government policies and are open to government scrutiny through bodies such as Regional Boards, Audit Commission, Communities Scotland, etc.

But the issue goes beyond formal lines of accountability and must also be about how we measure whether an organisation is doing what it claims it does. Accountability should not just be a paper exercise, but should involve direct challenges to processes. In a market we might suggest that things such as demand, price and profit can be seen as measures of effectiveness. In this way we can say consumers are getting what they want at a reasonable price, and that private businesses are doing well for their shareholders and staff.

But social housing is not simply a business and there are other concerns that we need to include, particularly regarding social and welfare issues. Therefore profit is not a particularly relevant consideration, and indeed choice might not be as important in social housing as in markets. We can explore this further by looking at the concept of value for money.

Value for money

This is essentially a means of determining that money is spent well and that it meets key aims and outcomes. Money will always be limited and thus decisions will have to be taken between competing interests. For example, do we prioritise provision for the elderly or for young single people? Do we improve one estate before the other, and how do we decide? In addition, there are always likely to be a range of stakeholders – applicants, tenants, staff, the local community, the taxpayer, etc. – and so decisions have to be made about whose priorities should prevail.

This raises the concept of *opportunity cost*. This is where the cost is conceived as the next best alternative opportunity foregone: if we had not decided to use the money for the agreed priority, what would we have done with it? As an example, we might judge expenditure on new social housing in terms of how many hospitals or schools we could have built with the money. So we can judge the manner in which we use resources by considering how else we might have used them.

What this suggests is that achieving value for money involves making the 'best' use of resources. This can never be an exact science, but Garnett and Perry (2005) argue that there are four means of measuring value for money. First, they point to the concept of *efficiency*. This is determined by considering the relationship between inputs and outputs. Efficiency relates to quantity – if we increase inputs, do outputs increase by at least as much? – and also to quality, in that we are interested in the quality of the houses we build and not just how many.

Efficiency is often used as a means to measure how well markets work, but we can question how far it fits in terms of welfare and socially based organisations. This is important in that efficiency has recently become a key term in judging housing organisations in England. This has proven to be a controversial issue, largely because of difficulties of comparison. For example, how do we compare the efficiency of a small association concentrating on supported housing and a large national association that provides a full range of services? Their management costs will differ, as will their staff/dwelling ratios. But just because the smaller association appears to be much more expensive per dwelling does this mean it is doing a worse job than the larger, apparently more efficient association?

This brings us to the concept of *effectiveness*, which is where we are concerned not merely with the quantity and quality of outputs, but also with their impact. It is where we seek to assess how outputs contribute to the key objectives and expectations of those with a legitimate interest. A problem here is that these interests may clash and so we need some means of prioritising them. This relates back to the general issue of who identifies the opportunity cost, and how we arrive at some consensus on this.

Another problem, particularly when dealing with long-lived assets like housing, is that we cannot measure effectiveness immediately but only over time. As an example, tower blocks built in the 1960s might have dealt with an immediate shortage of housing, but we might now question their effectiveness because of their higher maintenance costs, high voids and their general unpopularity. It therefore might now represent value for money to demolish them.

Third, Garnett and Perry (2005) point to the issue of equity. This relates to who benefits from a service and where the burdens of paying for it fall. Public bodies have to be demonstrably fair in how they use resources. However, not all households are at the same level in terms of income and opportunities. Therefore, allocating resources equally will not necessarily be fair (we need to remember here that equity and fairness are not the same as equality). When discussing school league tables, we often talk of measuring the 'value-added' impact of a policy rather than a more straightforward measure. A similar issue is presented by the example of the small specialist association discussed above: how do we measure the added value of a small number of expensive dwellings to a relatively small, but highly dependent, client group? Also the means we choose to fund activities such as major repairs and improvements is important here: do we charge the residents benefiting, or share the cost across the whole stock? Is it equitable that all residents pay for the improvements on only one estate? But then would it be fair to apportion the full cost to residents on that estate, many of whom might be unable to afford the increase?

The final means for determining value for money is by looking to *experience*. This relates to the expectations of the users and whether or not they perceive an improvement in the service. We might see this as the ultimate test, and in markets this can be easily measured by effective demand. In the public sector this might be measured by surveys and market research, but not so readily by changes in behaviour. One means of judging this in social housing might be through issues like voids and turnover, which can be taken to be indicators of poor quality.

What the issue of value for money does not settle, however, is whose perception is dominant. Should we take the voice of the tenants as being of greater importance than the local community, or the taxpayer as represented by government? In the UK we can say unequivocally that the dominant voice is that of government. Indeed even when there are attempts to 'empower' tenants and give them a voice, this is a requirement imposed on social landlords by government. The flow of accountability is therefore very much upwards to government rather than downwards to tenants. Accountability is thus very much tied up with the issue of control.

Controlling social housing

We can now turn to consider the manner in which government is able to control social housing and the mechanisms it uses to achieve this. What we shall seek to do is demonstrate the means by which government can control social housing and what pressures this places on landlords. One result of these pressures is a reduction in the distinction between local authorities and housing associations. This is partly due to stock transfer and the growth of the housing association sector. But it is also because central government has sought to control both sectors with common methods. Accordingly, for much of the discussion below we shall refer to social landlords and will only be more specific when necessary.

All governments like to suggest that they are being consistent, that their thinking and policy making is all 'joined-up' and that they have a clear way forward. In England it is certainly possible to see policies as being linked by some common purpose. The government suggests that this purpose is to improve the quality of social housing and to allow for greater choice and opportunity in the sector. Accordingly, they have introduced a number of policies regarding rents, quality of housing and the reform of Housing Benefit. Some of these policies, particularly regarding quality and Housing Benefit, also impact on Scotland and Wales. But there is also a different, more implicit purpose, which is to ensure that government maintains control over social housing and can thereby achieve its objectives without any adverse effects on the public purse.

Of course, it is rather easy to see patterns and suggest that it is all part of some grand plan. However, in this case, the government is quite explicit that these policies are linked, and indeed many of them have developed as a result of the 2000 Housing Green Paper (DETR, 2000). This does not mean that the policies will succeed in their intentions, but we should take the government's intentions at face value. So we shall look at these policies and how they link together.

Rent setting

In England a national rent setting policy was established in 2002. It should be seen, amongst other things, as a form of administrative rent control, in that it sets target rents that social landlords have to achieve by 2012. It is a rather prescriptive policy and has the effect of controlling the income of social landlords.

Rent restructuring can be seen as an attempt to restrict rent increases. However, it also aims to achieve some comparability across all social landlords in a locality. The government argues that 'choice in social housing is distorted when rents differ for no good reason' (DETR, 2000, p. 5). One of the aims of the policy, therefore, is to 'reduce unjustifiable differences between the rents set by local authorities and by registered social landlords' (DETR, 2000, p. 93), presumably so that applicants can make informed decisions. Housing association rents in 2000 were on average 20 per cent higher than those of local authorities, and the government felt that there should be some convergence. Moreover, they felt that rents should be set in both sectors, according to the same principles and using a formula combining property values and local earnings. A social landlord must calculate a target rent for each property with 70 per cent based on local earnings and the remaining 30 per cent based on local property values. The formula is geared to take account of bedroom size.

Landlords were given 10 years to move rents from the 2001/02 level to the target rent, using the formula of RPI+0.5 per cent. In addition to this formula they can apply a maximum £2 per week increase/decrease that shifts them towards the target.

Once social housing rents are comparable within a district, applicants, it is argued, will then be able to make comparisons between local social landlords in terms of quality and management rather than costs that have arisen as a result of different subsidy systems and rent setting policies. However, the logic of rent convergence is that target setting will remain after 2012 to ensure rents do not diverge.

The importance of the use of target rents with a cut-off date to achieve convergence means that social landlords now have a particularly clear notion of their income until 2012. This is one side of what can be seen as a pincer effect whereby social landlords are forced down particular routes by the policy mechanisms the government uses to control them.

Rent restructuring was not introduced in Scotland and so social landlords have greater discretion about rent setting within the general principle that rents should be affordable. However, the Scottish Government published research in late 2007 on the implications of a national approach to rent setting (Wilcox *et al.*, 2007). This review was seen as necessary because there was no firm guidance on affordability and a consequent feeling that not all

Think point

Consider what might be the advantages and disadvantages of a national rent setting policy. Who might benefit most from it: tenants, landlords or government?

social landlords were equally committed to affordability. In addition, the Scottish Government noted that the possible introduction of Housing Benefit reform by the UK government (this is a non-devolved area of policy) would have consequences for rents. The current position in Scotland, however, is that landlords retain greater flexibility in rent setting and therefore over their income as a whole.

Quality

The other side of the housing finance pincer in England, which affects the expenditure side, is the Decent Homes Standard. Like rent restructuring, this is a policy that affects the behaviour of social landlords in the long term by setting their priorities towards stock improvement above all other areas of activity. In effect, the prescriptions laid down by the Decent Homes Standard inform social landlords of their obligations in terms of dwelling standards and quantify the cost of improvements needed to attain this standard. As we saw in chapter 2, to meet the Decent Homes Standard each dwelling must:

- meet the current statutory minimum standard for housing;
- be in a reasonable state of repair;
- have reasonably modern facilities and services (age of bathroom, kitchen, etc.);
- provide a reasonable degree of thermal comfort (efficient heating and effective insulation).

In many ways this is the key component in the government's strategy for social housing in that achieving the Standard by 2010 has driven the decision making of social landlords. The starting point of the policy is for landlords to inspect and value their stock. As a result landlords are now able to apply a benchmark to their stock in terms of current valuation and survey data, and to relate this to the government's expectations of what standards ought to be. They are therefore able to cost the necessary remedial action needed to meet the standard. The Decent Homes Standard, taken together with rent restructuring, means that the government now exercises considerable control over the activities of social landlords and is able to determine both income and expenditure.

Both Scotland and Wales have their own quality standards. Scotland has the Scottish Housing Quality Standard (SHQS), which was introduced in 2004 and has a target of 2015. The criteria for the standard are similar to that in England, but more extensive. Social dwellings in Scotland should be:

- compliant with the tolerable standard;
- free from serious disrepair;
- energy efficient;
- provided with modern facilities and services;
- healthy, safe and secure.

There is therefore a greater commitment in the Scottish standard to energy efficiency.

The Welsh Assembly has adopted the Welsh Housing Quality Standard with a target of compliance by 2012. This standard is rather more extensive than those in England and Scotland and requires that a dwelling:

- is in a good state of repair;
- is safe and secure;
- is adequately heated, fuel efficient and well insulated;
- contains up-to-date kitchens and bathrooms;
- is well managed;
- is located in attractive and safe environments;
- suits the specific requirements of the households in terms of special needs.

Whilst this is more onerous, it is also more open to interpretation, particularly those points relating to good management and the general environment. Indeed, it is interesting that the Welsh standard seeks to look at issues beyond the dwelling. This suggests an attempt to link the quality of housing to wider issues than the physical amenities of the property.

What is clear, though, is that the quality of social housing is a central concern and this is where resources are being targeted. This explains why social housing building since 2000 has been at historically low levels in the UK, despite an increase in government expenditure as compared with the 1990s. Relatively fewer resources are being targeted at new development in order to allow social landlords to bring their existing dwellings up to the requisite standard.

Think point

Should all social housing be up to a common quality standard, or should it be left to landlords to decide? If some households would prefer cheaper housing, even if it were to a lower standard, why should they not have it?

The pressure to improve standards has also been one of the driving forces to stock transfer, particularly in England where rent restructuring also applies. Central government has largely dictated income and expenditure for social landlords. But this pressure is only heightened by a further mechanism.

Resource accounting

This policy was introduced by the Treasury across the UK in 2001 and can be seen as attempting several things. First, it recognises officially what had long been the reality, that the role of local authorities had now changed to that of managers and maintainers rather than developers of housing. Central government since the 1980s had discouraged local authorities from building by the way it set priorities and targets and allocated resources. Resource accounting recognised this by shifting the emphasis away from historic debt incurred in asset formation (the cost of housebuilding) to a form of accounting that records the current value of their assets. This means that each authority has to be aware of the condition of their housing stock and the amount of money needed to improve it. Resource accounting can be seen as an attempt to 'measure on a consistent basis the resources used over the lifetime of houses, rather than simply the cash spent on them each year' (Malpass and Aughton, 1999, p. 34).

The government intends that resource accounting will make local authorities more businesslike in their operation and encourage them to manage their assets more effectively. Accordingly, they are now expected to submit annual business plans for their housing revenue account. These plans will indicate how the authority intends to use and enhance its assets over a period of up to 30 years. Indeed the political aim of business planning is to ensure that local authorities are clear about the nature and scale of the problems facing them and what options are available to them. It forces local authorities to concentrate on long-term planning and the need to maintain and improve their own stock, and in particular, of course, to show how they intend to meet the Decent Homes Standard.

In Scotland, local authorities have to prepare a delivery plan showing how they expect to meet the Scottish Housing Quality Standard by 2015. Likewise, in Wales local authorities have been required to undertake business planning to assess the resources needed to meet their quality standard.

It is the need for long-term planning that is the really significant part of the policy, and this becomes clear when we link it to the previous two policies. The limitations of rent restructuring mean that English local authorities know what income they have at their disposal until 2012. The Decent Homes Standard informs them of what they must do to improve their assets by 2010. There is therefore no possibility for ignorance on the part of landlords about the scale of the problems facing them. For many local authorities this means a deficit between their projected income and their necessary expenditure. They are therefore forced to consider means of addressing this shortfall, and for many of them this has involved stock transfer.

Stock transfer is clearly the government's preferred option for social housing. The effects of business planning, and the control of income and expenditure, have exerted pressure on local authorities to make fundamental decisions in the knowledge that most will not receive sufficient resources to meet the Decent Homes Standard by 2010. The effect is that much of the cost of stock improvements is therefore funded privately, but without any diminution of government regulation.

These mechanisms are all very prescriptive and intrusive and have a direct impact on the day-to-day operation of social landlords. Any sense in which the stock of social housing is still a local asset has been lost. But it is also important to note that government seeks to achieve this control without having ownership of the stock. Indeed one of the principal effects of its policies is to 'privatise' council housing. Its control over finance and the subsidy system means that owning the stock is no longer necessary: rent restructuring and the Decent Homes Standard apply equally to both local authorities and housing associations. The effects of these mechanisms are highlighted in Table 6.2.

This is perhaps the major paradox of housing policy over the last two decades: that running parallel with policies aimed at inculcating choice and

Table 6.2   How government controls social housing in England

- Rent restructuring controls income.
- Decent Homes Standard controls expenditure.
- Business planning makes social landlords consider their options and makes any deficit in income evident.
- All options to make good the deficit involve using private finance.

Think point

Should central government control social housing or should it be left to local communities? What are the financial advantages and disadvantages of centralisation?

personal responsibility we have seen more prescriptive control over the finance and management of social housing (King, 2006). Indeed the structure that government has created is such that it exercises control over the income and expenditure of social landlords, even as it engineered the situation in which new social housing can only be built through the increasing use of private finance.

Private finance

Since 1989 there has been a significant increase in the use of private finance to help fund social housing in all parts of the UK. This has mainly taken the form of private borrowing by housing associations and through stock transfer, whereby local authority housing stock is sold to a new housing association set up for the purpose, which has borrowed money to finance the transaction and to fund repairs and improvements.

Of course, in the private rented and owner occupation sectors, using private finance has been the norm. Whilst both sectors have received some government support, the main means of funding have been a landlord's or household's own resources, or through borrowing from private sources. So we can say that private finance is hardly new to housing provision when 80 per cent of UK dwellings have been built or are maintained using private finance. We should also bear in mind that the overwhelming majority of social housing has been built by private companies under contract to local authorities and housing associations.

We can argue that housing policy since the late 1980s has depended on private finance in order to meet successive governments' aims. The scale of private finance is now quite large, with England seeing an injection of at least £26 billion into social housing between 1989 and 2005. This is more than the amount of government expenditure on housing associations in this period, which stands at £24 billion (Wilcox, 2008). Private finance has there-fore allowed for a doubling of housing association activity over and above what it would have been if it had relied solely on government funding. In Scotland, the amount of private finance raised by housing associations from 1989 to 2006 is well over £2 billion, accounting for about a third of total capital investment in the period (Wilcox, 2008).

So the first reason for this policy is that it allowed for an expansion of activity without huge extra costs to government. Hence government, par-ticularly in the 1990s, could maintain tight public spending policies whilst increasing the actual level of outputs. Particularly important in this regard is that borrowing by housing associations does not count as public borrow-ing, and thus does not add to the public debt. Local authority borrowing, however, is treated as public debt and so is tightly controlled by central government.

There are, of course, more overtly political or ideological issues at play here. Governments since the late 1970s have looked to limit the size of the public sector and have further sought to use private sector disciplines as a spur to efficiency. Government has sought to transfer the risk away from the Treasury and onto to the providers themselves. Private finance, with the need to provide security against assets and ensure debts are repaid, is one means of sharing risk (DOE, 1987).

It was also argued that a more commercial orientation would ensure greater value for money and efficiency. Social providers would have to be more cost conscious and businesslike in their approach. They would be encouraged to plan more for the long term because they were now committed to long-term debt financing. It was believed that disciplines of private business would improve the way public bureaucracies operated and deal with some of the problems discussed above regarding public bodies. Entrepreneurialism and competition were therefore to be encouraged, and private finance would enforce this on social landlords. In particular, the Private Finance Initiative (PFI), or what are sometimes referred to as Public–Private Partnerships (PPPs), has been extensively used across the public sector, particularly in health and transport.

Think point

What would have happened to social housing since 1990 without private finance?

Funding new social housing

So the basis of the funding system for social housing is access to private finance. In order for housing associations to develop, they need to raise the difference between a predetermined grant and the total cost of development from private institutions, such as building societies and banks. Moreover, throughout the 1990s the grant rate in England was consistently reduced from 75 per cent in 1989 to 52 per cent in 1998. As a result, the proportion of private finance needed to be increased. In addition, the grant rate was a national average and therefore for most areas outside London the grant rate was lower. For example, in the late 1990s housing associations in the East

Midlands were developing with grant rates as low as 20–25 per cent. The average grant rate was increased to 68 per cent in 2002 to ensure that associations could continue to develop under rent restructuring. However, the total amount of grant was not increased in proportion, with the effect that the number of dwellings produced declined.

In England, under the funding regime of the Housing Corporation,[1] known as the National Affordable Housing Programme (NAHP), specific grant rates have been abolished. Funding is allocated through the NAHP on the basis of bids received from housing associations. The majority of funding is allocated to so-called *investment partners*, who are accredited by the Corporation as capable of helping it to fulfil its strategic aims. Bids are assessed according to the following criteria:

- value in terms of public subsidy per home and per person housed;
- quality judged using the Corporation's design and quality standards;
- deliverability with particular concern for planning status;
- policy fit with national, regional and local strategies.

In Scotland funding for housing associations has been managed through Communities Scotland's affordable housing investment programme. This system also requires private finance, with Communities Scotland providing Housing Association Grant. Grant rates in Scotland have typically been higher than in England, never falling below 65 per cent for the country as a whole since 1989. In Wales housing associations are funded through the Welsh Assembly Government, again using a mix of social housing grant and private finance.

In general, until the financial crisis in 2008 associations have had no difficulty in raising all the private finance they have needed to fund new developments. Indeed there has been a reasonably competitive market that has developed to cater for their finance requirements. Interest rates have been at historically low levels and financial institutions have been relatively ready to invest. We should also note that from the investors' perspective lending on housing development, which is partly subsidised by government, presents a lower risk than a purely commercial transaction. We can speculate whether this benign situation can be maintained if the 'credit crunch' continues much beyond 2008. In circumstances of restricted bank lending some associations will certainly find it difficult to finance their activities.

However, generally, we can suggest that the housing association private finance market depends on three factors. First, there is a need for consistency in government policy on issues such as grants, rents and Housing Benefit entitlement. As an example, the introduction of rent restructuring has reduced the flexibility an association might have to deal with financial crises, in that it cannot increase its rents to pay off its creditors. Second, changes in the financial markets, particularly moves in interest rates over the period of the loan, can have an impact. This is particularly so as many loans were initially on a low start basis, which made them more affordable in the early years but which need real term rent increases to fund higher repayments towards the end of the period. The third issue is the state of alternative markets. Both the commercial and domestic property markets are much larger and more established markets. The housing association market will remain small and specialised, but is relatively safe so long as government offers subsidies to limit the amount of private finance needed.

The impact of private finance has been considerable. Not only has it moved the culture and ethos of associations away from a welfare orientation and towards a more commercial approach, it has also led to mergers, take-overs and expansions so that the number of developing associations has reduced dramatically since 1990. The advent of the Sustainable Communities Plan (see chapter 5) has speeded up this progress, with its emphasis on partnership working and the restriction of funding to only a small number of large players. Likewise, the need for investment partnerships emphasises both the capacity for relatively large-scale development and a proven track record of performance.

The overall picture in Scotland shows some important differences from the English context. There has been a much stronger attachment to community-based housing associations and there is a rather higher proportion of small organisations than in England. Mergers and take-overs have been rather less significant forces, although managerialism and the business focus have played important roles in shaping the sector's outlook. Since the mid-2000s, however, Scotland too has turned to investing more in larger organisations and consortia.

Another significant effect of the use of private finance has been to increase rents. Wilcox (2005) showed that in the first 15 years of private finance housing association rents in England increased from an average of £24.50 per week in 1989 to £60.33 in 2004. This has added to problems of affordability, particularly for households in low paid employment. This has had a knock-on effect on Housing Benefit, in that 53 per cent of housing association tenants were on Housing Benefit in 1989 compared with 67 per cent in 2005 (Wilcox, 2008). What this shows is that, whilst associations might have become more businesslike, they are still very dependent on public subsidy. Indeed, as we argued in chapter 5, they have used Housing Benefit as a means of offsetting reductions in Social Housing Grant in England and Housing Association Grant in Scotland.

Think point

Who benefits from private finance?

Whilst private finance has become an established part of housing finance, it is not immune to criticism (summarised in Table 6.3). Most obviously, we might argue that it is inappropriate for the profit motive to drive the actions of leading players in social and welfare provision. Helping people in severe housing need should not be turned into a profit-making venture. Money that could be going to services is instead going to shareholders and 'fat cat' salaries. However, as we have already mentioned, nearly all social housing has been built by private companies who expected to make a profit from it (as did those developers building schools and hospitals).

Second, it might be argued that private finance, either because of the need to return a profit or merely because of the risks involved, is more expensive than traditional forms of management and provision. Whilst it may appear a cheaper option now, we – and our children – will be paying an excessive amount for these housing, road and other infrastructure projects well into the future. This is a particular criticism often thrown at PFI schemes, which have increasingly been used to fund new capital projects like roads, hospitals and schools. Instead of government paying the full capital cost upfront, a PFI involves contracting a private firm to build and manage the new asset in return for a fixed payment over the life of the contract. These capital projects remain 'off balance sheet' and so do not contribute to government debt. Government then funds them by additional revenue support. This means that a fixed amount of funding per year sees many more capital projects built immediately than if government funded them upfront.

However, merely because the costs are somewhat hidden, this does not make them go away. What makes this an issue is that, whilst these hospitals,

Table 6.3   Objections to private finance

- It is inappropriate to make a profit from social provision.
- Using measures like the Private Finance Initiative is more expensive than direct government provision.
- Private provision loses the democratic control of services.
- End to local ownership.

schools or housing schemes are built privately, it is inconceivable that government would allow the services to be closed if the contractor were to collapse. This indeed happened in 2006, when a company contracted to upgrade parts of the London Underground went bankrupt. This service was too important to the economy to be shut down and so government had to intervene to help find an alternative.

Third, we can suggest that much of the move to private finance involves the loss of public and democratic control. It is often criticised for being a form of privatisation that places private interest above those of the general public. Finally, we might argue that the rush to develop group structures and mergers as a result of the imperative imposed by private finance has created considerable upheaval at the local level. We are starting to see a shift away from local decision making and a reduction in diversity, as groups share 'best practice' across their structure. Accordingly, locally based associations are starting to lose their identity. What increasingly drives decision making within associations is not local issues or even housing-based issues, but financial, legal and investment decisions, which, in turn, are all linked to the national policy agenda.

Think point

Does it matter who owns social housing as long as there is sufficient funding to build and manage good quality dwellings?

What is the future role of social housing?

We have seen that government seems more concerned with the control of social housing than encouraging it, and that even the use of commercial disciplines and private finance does not mean any diminution in this control. When we combine this situation with the discussion on housing allowances in chapter 5 we can start to piece together some of the incentives that operate in the sector, and how it relates to other tenures. These relationships are quite complex, but we can see a pattern in which one aspect of policy is being used to mask the risks posed by another.

As an example we can look at the operation of Housing Benefit as it currently stands. The direct payment of Housing Benefit to social landlords means that claimants are effectively 'tagged' and have a distinct value over and above those in work. This is because the landlord has a guaranteed income from accepting these tenants. But the reverse applies in the private rented sector as a result of the new local housing allowance that is paid directly to tenants. Ignoring the issue of equitable treatment between tenures, this might not matter if social housing were able to house all those in housing need and the private rented sector were only housing those who had a range of choices. This, however, is not the case and many low priority households, such as childless couples and single persons, have to rely on the private rented sector if owner occupation is unaffordable for them.

This situation, however, does not mean that the social rented sector is being favoured, at least not in absolute terms. Social housing may receive more benefits than private renting, but it is still a poor relation when compared with owner occupation. In fact since the mid-1970s social housing has been in decline, with a reduction in stock and the quality of housing and an increase in social problems, such as anti-social behaviour and economic dependency. A number of reasons account for this situation, which are detailed in Table 6.4.

All the changes mentioned in Table 6.4 need to be seen within the context of the growth in owner occupation since the 1970s. The majority of households are owner occupiers and expect to remain so. The children of these households likewise confidently expect to become owners. As we saw in chapter 5, this focuses government's attention onto owner occupation and the need to encourage and support it. As with policies such as Homebuy, government is prepared to use social housing to support the majority tenure.

The problem is that social housing is not strong enough to withstand the onslaught from these changes. As a result it has become residualised and a tenure of last resort. The reasons it could not defend itself are reasonably

Table 6.4 Why social housing has become residualised

- Housing Benefit means that the very poorest are able to gain access to social housing.

- Homelessness legislation since 1977 has led to an increase in the number of vulnerable and workless households.

- Many of the most affluent households have left the sector due to the Right to Buy, taking many of the family houses with them.

- The reduction in government spending since the late 1970s has meant that much of the lost stock could not be replaced.

- Centralisation has had the cumulative effect of stifling innovation and homogenising the tenure through so-called 'best practice'.

clear. Social housing was never the majority tenure (apart from a period of time in Scotland) and so it has never dominated. There have always been more people who were not social tenants. Over time, as owner occupation has increased, this disparity has grown larger, such that social housing is beyond the experience of most people and does not fit in with their aspirations. Added to this, social housing is particularist, rather than universalist as health and education are, and this is a key distinction in terms of its political significance and its importance as a key electoral issue.

This decline in social housing becomes self-perpetuating, particularly in the growing distinction between those who pay for a benefit and those who receive it. This is an inevitable consequence of means testing, which creates a situation in which an increasing number of social tenants do not contribute to tax revenues, and those paying tax do not get, or even want, access to social housing.

We also need to be aware of the ideological and cultural significance of individualism in England in particular (Macfarlane, 1978). This idea of individualism is most commonly expressed in the cliché 'An Englishman's home is his castle' and, like most clichés, it carries within it a certain amount of truth. Britain, as with many developed countries, has become more individualist and this is represented by the appeal of property ownership.

There are at least two controversial, but conflicting, conclusions we can come to. First, we might see social provision as a failed experiment, whereby it was hoped to increase the quality and supply of housing through state provision. Yet it failed because of the huge expense involved in mass house-building, the consequent restriction of access only to those in need, and, more recently, the resistance of a majority of households who have aspired to owner occupation. In other words, social housing was both unaffordable, and was a form of provision that could not deal with rising affluence and the expectations that flowed from that.

Alternatively, and no less controversially, we might see social housing as a temporary expedient to meet the problem of shortage. It was needed in the early part of the twentieth century as a means of helping the majority of the population to a high level of housing consumption. The emphasis therefore, quite properly, was on dealing with a problem of sufficient quantity. But towards the end of the century it was possible to return to a more market-based system of provision, as had been the case before 1914. Social housing was therefore just a means of improving housing conditions; but once there was a crude surplus of dwellings the emphasis could shift elsewhere. Were we to see social housing not as an experiment, but as a time-limited mechanism to reinvigorate markets, then it need not be seen as a failure, but rather as a service whose useful life may now be over.

Of course we could take the simple and straightforward view that social housing was about rising living standards and helping the poorest and that there was nothing more to its development than that. But there are a number of reasons for this being too simplistic. First, as we have seen, until the 1970s social housing did not help the very poorest, but aided those with a secure income. It was not until the introduction of Housing Benefit in 1972 that the poorest could gain access. Second, we can challenge whether social housing has actually always been high quality provision. The history of social housing development particularly in urban areas from the 1950s onwards was not always particularly a happy one (Power, 1987, 1993). We should also note that since the late 1980s there has been a plethora of policies aimed at improving and rehabilitating social housing. This has culminated in the Decent Homes Standard, which targets resources on improving social housing. We can therefore argue that an increasing amount of housing subsidies are being used to deal with the consequences of past subsidies, and so the quality of social housing can be questioned.

Third, social housing did not raise people out of poverty, but tended to concentrate them in one place. Until the 1970s it excluded the poor and so they congregated in poor quality private housing. In this period it actually helped more affluent households have access to better quality housing and eventually to buy their dwelling through the Right to Buy, even though they might actually have been able to buy in the open market. Later, social housing became dominated by the poorest households dependent on benefits.

But what does all this say about the future of social housing? If the problem is a cultural one, we might suggest that the prognosis must be bleak. Perhaps the only way to achieve any resurgence in social housing would be some major catastrophe in the housing market that goes beyond any of the depressions of the last 50 years. After all, we can state that owner occupation has thrived at the expense of social housing, so why not the reverse? But this would have to be a major cataclysm involving mass repossessions and a huge change in perceptions about the virtues of ownership. But why would we wish for this? And in any case, we can hardly plan for it. If the experience of the bank bailouts in the USA, UK and Europe in 2008 are any guide, we can expect government to go very far indeed to support the housing market. We can therefore state that a cataclysm is untenable. And, of course, this presupposes that there would be a mass shift in attitudes towards owning.

This raises a very real problem about attitudes toward social housing and the possibility of change. This is that, outside the housing profession and a few representative and campaigning bodies, there appears to be very little demand for change. The majority of households do not see it as a desirable tenure, and this reduces the clamour for change. It might be harsh to state that the poor have less of a voice, but experience of democratic politics in the era of mass owner occupation seems to suggest that it is true.

We might actually say that it is the very structure of social provision that has created this lack of voice. It is the very targeting of social housing for the benefit of particular groups that creates marginalisation and separation from the mainstream. It is a policy that is demonstrably self-fulfilling, in that the majority feel that social housing is neither intended for them nor does it have any particular appeal. Government might want to create more diverse communities that are not dominated by economically dependent households, but it is difficult to see how such policies can flourish within a tenure that explicitly focuses on the vulnerable. If governments are genuinely serious about creating diversity, this necessitates the downgrading of need and vulnerability as the key access criteria and allowing more affluent households to enter the tenure. But this would open policy makers up to the accusation that they are benefiting the more affluent at the expense of the poor.

There is a genuine dilemma here, that government cannot reform social housing without offering incentives to those who are not the most in need, and that it should do this at a time when social housing has to be rationed because of its relative scarcity. Whilst it proved acceptable to use social housing to assist households into owner occupation, this was largely because there was an expectation that households would be better off as a result. However, opening up social housing to those more affluent would be directly at the expense of the poorest. But, of course, the more affluent households are already more likely to be well housed and have more options available to them, and so might not need any more help.

This suggests that the future role of social housing is actually more of the same. It will continue to house the vulnerable and to be a minority, indeed declining, tenure. And whilst this is occurring we can also expect that the current culture of social housing will be maintained. In terms of this culture, what has been interesting is that, as social housing has declined and become more residualised, the sector has become ostensibly more commercial and businesslike. This has arisen because of the financial pressures imposed on social landlords, and so we can see it as the outcome of centralised control. Therefore, we need to conclude our look at social housing with an examination of this commercialisation.

Social housing and risk

Earlier in the chapter we saw that social housing had been altered by the use of what might be called commercial disciplines. However, I also suggested that one of the reasons that financial institutions have been prepared to lend to social landlords is that social house building is still subsidised, and so the risk to the lender is reduced. In addition, we have also seen that social landlords are able to 'capture' Housing Benefit to offset their exposure resulting from private finance. The situation with regard to risk and commercialisation is therefore a complex one.

We might suggest that the transformation of social housing into a more commercialised environment has been created by what might be called a *manufactured risk*, created by the reduction in state subsidy leading to a need to raise private finance for new housing development. But there has been no real change in the position of social landlords relative to their current or potential tenants. Landlords still hold the same power over them and control access and the terms of the relationship. The change has been a bureaucratic one involving their relations with government, its agencies and financial institutions.

We might even argue that the *pseudo-commercial* pressures on social landlords have diminished the choices of tenants through a concentration of housing stock in the hands of fewer large organisations. We saw that the funding system created incentives for mergers and take-overs resulting in an increase in the capability for volume building. Likewise, a policy such as choice-based lettings has led to a common allocations system within a local authority area, giving no possibility of opting out or using an alternative structure: an applicant has no choice but to play by the rules determined by a cartel of local landlords.

This means that from the tenants' perspective choice is a chimera, a mere apparition of change whereby the landlords still determine the level of choice according to government criteria and whereby landlords are forced to compete for government patronage and thus modify their behaviour to suit government. The result is a creeping homogeneity and uniformity. And perversely, the level of regulation and supervision has increased as government funding has decreased and narrowed: social landlords are controlled by regulation, even as their chances of receiving development funding are diminishing. All social landlords, whether they receive grant funding or not, are inspected, regulated and committed to fulfilling the Decent Homes Standard and rent restructuring.

We might see this situation as something of a trade-off. On the one hand, government needs the means to ensure that social housing declines gracefully, as it were, so that there is no struggle or conflict over how it is being treated. It is easier to gain control through compliance rather than conflict or through the courts. This can best be done through financial mechanisms that hem landlords in. But, on the other hand, commercialisation provides key decision makers within social housing with sufficient benefits and the justification that they are entrepreneurs and risk-takers, taking business decisions in a commercial environment. They deal with the Stock Exchange, banks and building societies, and use innovative financial products that give the appearance of being businesses. Hence there is the creation of a pseudo-entrepreneurial class of senior executives who have bought into the government's agenda and are being rewarded accordingly. Once this pseudo-entrepreneurialism has reached a critical mass, it can self-generate and become the standard for the sector to work to, apparently independent of government control. Indeed large social landlords have started to challenge the government's agenda and move outside it by working with private developers and looking to develop housing for sale themselves.

But, of course, the environment they operate in is relatively risk-free. They are backed by government and its regulators who would not allow the loss of social housing on any large scale. But more fundamentally their business development is predicated on a guaranteed rental stream through Housing Benefit, paid in most cases directly to the landlord. Hence, as we have seen in chapter 5, there has been a significant increase in Housing Benefit dependency on the part of social tenants from just over 46.5 per cent in 1996 to 67.1 per cent in 2007. The development may not have been consciously engineered by landlords; it may be a function of affordability, of relative desirability and (lack of) choice, but it has allowed for a significant amount of risk transference back to government. So we have the perversity of social landlords becoming more entrepreneurial on the back of increased benefit dependency.

Failure on the part of social landlords and senior executives would be damaging to them organisationally and personally, but it would have none of the consequences of a proper business, in terms of bankruptcy and liquidation. Nor would it impact particularly on customers, who would not see any difference in the management of their dwelling or rent levels as these are all determined by government targets and standards. Indeed, in most cases they would be cushioned by Housing Benefit from any upheaval. This also means, of course, that failure is likely to be due to incompetence or bureaucratic failure rather than being financially driven.

This pseudo-commercialism also makes no real difference to the manner in which social housing is viewed by the general public, and nor does it impact, either positively or negatively, on the position of the tenure relative to owner occupation. This is because those outside the sector only see the product and not the internal processes. Social housing appears the same, whether its outputs are the result of successful business planning or pure chance. It appears no more or less attractive and its position in relation to owner occupation is unaffected.

A final, but important, point is that the pseudo-commercialisation of social housing means that the key relationships that social landlords have are with other organisations and not their tenants. Because of benefit dependency it is all too easy to take tenants for granted as passive recipients, whose rent is paid on their behalf and who can be offered safe choices. Thus both landlord and tenant can live risk-free, without undue concern for the consequences of their actions.

Think point

Does it make any sense to see social landlords as businesses?

Conclusions

In this chapter we have discussed how government seeks to control social provision. We have seen that the level of control is pervasive and its effects have been considerable. Government has been able to maintain a high degree of control, whilst also apparently introducing a more commercial environment into social housing. However, we have also seen that this commercialism has been enforced from above and that it is supported by the existence of subject subsidies, which have been captured by social landlords.

We can view this in one of two ways. We can suggest that both government and social landlords are cynical manipulators, seeking to benefit politically or materially from the system they operate within. Alternatively, we can assume that all the players at the various levels are honest and working with the best of intentions. We have no evidence or reason to suggest that people are acting cynically, even though it might be a convenient explanation. Therefore we ought to take the actions of government and social landlords at face value and assume their integrity.

But, of course, this makes any explanation of what has happened more complicated and difficult both to make and accept. However, I believe that we can return to some of the basic premises we discussed in the opening chapter of this book, and which we have reiterated periodically throughout the ensuing chapters. Housing finance systems are dynamic and open, such that they are constantly evolving because of internal and external pressures that impact on the incentive structures of the various players within the system. The result is that there are unforeseen and unintended consequences, and all of this is due to individuals and organisations operating from the best of motives in trying to achieve their aims. Many of these aims are explicit and open, but some are implicit and so we can only surmise and speculate on the motivations involved.

Indeed much of the latter part of this chapter has been somewhat speculative and based on a particular understanding of how housing finance has impacted on one particular system. But it is possible to generalise from this discussion to show the importance of understanding the complexity of systems and the role played by incentives within dynamic structures.

Further reading

A much more detailed and comprehensive coverage of UK social housing finance can be found in Garnett and Perry (2005). A critical discussion of social housing can be found in my book, *Choice and the End of Social Housing* (2006). A very different take on social housing, but also critical of the direction of policy, can be found in Malpass (2005).

7

Complexity and choice

Learning outcomes

- Complexity means that governments mainly react rather than plan actions.
- Markets and governments have distinct functions that need to be kept separate.
- There is a need to recognise the limits of our understanding of markets and act accordingly.

Having considered housing finance, and made a pitch for how it can and should be understood, I want now to put forward a particular position. This position is precisely about *understanding* housing finance, about how it appears and what we should make of it. This involves raking up some of the key arguments, but not in any formal way or with a view to summarising the arguments made in this book.

What I have tried to do is to develop an appreciation of the importance of certain concepts, such as quality, access, need, choice and responsibility; from these human motivations and basic requirements we have built formal structures that help us to understand housing finance. We have seen that often these structures have arisen in a non-purposive manner, through interaction in markets rather than through deliberate construction; hence the importance of ideas such as the invisible hand and unintended consequences.

The complexity of the relationships involved makes them difficult to understand. Indeed there is something of a paradox in understanding complexity. We might appreciate that complexity is an issue and that we need to account for it in our understanding of housing finance; yet things are just so complex that we simply cannot hope to understand them in all their detail. So if we can never fully understand systems, what limit does this place on policy making? If we can never understand fully, should we even try? But, of course, if we do not try to understand more, we will never do better.

What we have to understand is that complexity means that governments, despite their rhetoric, are largely only able to react to situations. They can only respond to markets, this being in the nature of the relationship between a constructivist and evolutionary rationality. Markets develop in a non-predictive, non-patterned manner, yet government is constituted formally as a definitive structural entity. Government is just not nimble enough to deal with the dynamic nature of markets.

But this does not mean that government lacks the ambition. In particular, it increasingly uses market disciplines, ideas and concepts to control and reform its own agencies. We need to understand why this has occurred: is it cyclical? Might we be in a 'market phase' and so at some time in the future expect to shift to a 'state phase'? Or is there now some genuine recognition of markets as the most effective form of social organisation, of the efficacy of the price mechanism, the importance of incentives, the desire to own things? A market-based system is capable of delivering all of these, and government, however benign it might appear to be, simply fails to provide them. Or is it that the market is simply the default position? Is it what we get if there is no government intervention? Do we have some recognition that markets are 'natural' (in the particular sense of anything created by human action is natural, in that it is not purposively designed but derives out of what humans do when they relate to others)? If government wishes to offer incentives, it introduces risk and competition as in a market. If government wishes to offer people choices and to help them to achieve their aspirations, it does this through the encouragement of ownership and personal decision making, again just as in a market where consumers have choices over their assets.

But perversely, when a modern government does these things, as in Britain and parts of Europe, this does not have the effect of reducing the power of the state, and this must lead us to question the real extent of these changes. So how far does risk and competition really exist? How much choice do users of public services really have? What incentives are there, particularly for those in receipt of social housing and welfare benefits? Is not the problem here that government wants the benefits of markets, but without relinquishing any of its controls? It still wants to determine outcomes. Indeed it has already set the outcomes and is simply using market disciplines as a means to achieve these. It therefore has little or no conception of unintended consequences or the sense that a market acts as if an invisible hand is operating. Government only wants certain aspects of markets, and it requires them to be consistent and contained. Yet, in doing so, it has not really grasped the complexity or the subtlety of market provision, in particular the idea that outcomes are not given and predictable, or that outcomes are in any way compatible with a pre-planned political agenda seeking to promote notions, like fairness, decent housing for all or social justice. A market cannot guarantee these things, and this means either government action, if it is genuinely based on market disciplines, fails, or that the market mechanisms created by government are artificial and rigged to achieve certain outcomes.

But this will also end in failure because the ends are simply incompatible with the means. There can be no accommodation with the two forms of rationality identified by Hayek (1978): we cannot use evolutionary rationality for constructivist purposes. The result would simply be a purposive construction. Evolution cannot be pre-formed or pre-programmed; we cannot cheat just to get the outcome we desire.

So government seeks to understand markets, but not, we might say, with the requisite humility. It sees 'the' market still as an entity, as a thing with particular properties, a framework perhaps to be imposed on a willing and compliant public sector, which is then capable of assured results. Government is, though, too glib about what it will get from its adventures with markets. There can be no real predictability when people are allowed real choices to meet their aspirations, if only because these aspirations are not uniform or even necessarily coherent. The only means to achieve a predictable outcome is to attenuate the choices that are possible. So, for example, we cannot open up social provision to market level rents and expect nothing else to change; and neither can we control rents without altering the incentive structure of both landlords and tenants.

Offering choices affects our expectations, but these are not readily measurable. And once we have those expectations, they will not then go away. We do not unlearn or forget what we can have and have been told we are meant to have. The problem then is one of continued centralised control from government within conditions of rising expectations. This is why government can do more, yet be accused of doing less or not enough, as is the case within the UK housing market in 2008 and has been the case with health care for the last few years. Expectations have outstripped the government's ability to manage them, even when it has doubled spending on health care in less than a decade. Government is trying to have both a market-based system and centralised government control. But this is really not possible, and it is the market element that will suffer because we cannot have both concurrently. Government cannot set the outcomes and try to manage the incentive structures *and* give individuals choice and organisations the freedom to compete and to set their own objectives.

Does this mean that government fails? If we wish to judge according to markets and individual choices, then clearly it does. But government does not actually fail often and this is because it is the one doing the testing and the judging. By its own lights government does not fail, and this is because the means of success are internal to government: they are based around its control over resources and meeting the targets it has set. Government therefore does not often allow itself to fail. And so, if we judge success in these terms – by green papers, policy documents and targets – we can suggest that government does succeed. But in the UK in 2008 there was a government claiming success in terms of meeting its housebuilding targets and the soundness of the economy, even if things are more difficult. However, at the same time as this boasting is going on, there had been a run on a major bank, leading to its nationalisation, an emergency budget making tax changes to help the low paid only ten weeks after the official Budget, forecasts of significant falls in house prices of anything up to 20 per cent, and then the virtual collapse of mortgage lending. Yet if the measure of success is house-building targets with an end date of 2020, then things are still on target: in 2008 how can they not be? But if we look outside the government's sights and towards the actual market conditions, where most people go for their housing, then things look rather different. What this episode in contemporary history shows is that government often does not understand markets despite all the resources it can bring to bear.

This, of course, is not to suggest that markets are perfect, that they work well, nor that people do not suffer real hardship because of changes in markets. But this is precisely the problem with government's use of market disciplines. It can only use market disciplines and mechanisms on the premise that they are always beneficial. Government cannot countenance the downside, that prices can go down, as well as up, that assets might turn into liabilities, that there are as many, if not more, losers as winners. Competition means someone coming second, or even last; choice means that some will take bad decisions and end up poor or destitute or under threat; unintended consequences mean that things *will* go wrong and fingers will be pointed at those held to blame. Yet government cannot admit this, that its policies are designed to make some people fail and end up worse off; that organisations will fail and go bankrupt because of government design, and that this is just the way the world is. Choice and competition can only be portrayed as beneficial and for the best and that everyone therefore will inevitably be better off.

The result of this lack of understanding is attenuated choices; 'safe' choices where failure is not permitted or compensated for. In reality choice becomes merely just another means of bureaucratic allocation (Brown and King, 2005), a means of allocating scarce resources where the same people

– the vulnerable, those most in need – are chosen by the landlord, so long as they bid, co-operate with the landlord and go through the pantomime of choosing. And risk is consequence free because decisions are backed by subsidies, by the landlord's ability to choose those applicants who come with a subsidy attached.

There is then, we might conclude, a lack of honesty in housing finance policy, involving the improper use of markets to meet the ends of government. And, of course, this means the either/ors we began with – of needs and choice; markets and government – have not really gone away. Yes, markets and government are interlinked and needs can be instrumental to the choices we have made, but the relationship is not symbiotic; it is not mutual and strengthening for both sides. Rather the relationship between markets and government is parasitic, in which government strangles the life out of markets. Markets work best where government is relatively weak and sticks to doing only what it has to do.

Now it may well be that a situation could arise in which markets use government – there are, after all, often complaints of this, about who benefits from planning and from government contracts, of government 'being in bed' with private developers, the large supermarket chains and big business. It may be the case that large businesses are indeed taking advantage of government's naiveté and lack of proper understanding of markets. But 'big business' is not the same as markets; rather they are monopolists or oligopolists with market power who are sufficiently well organised to benefit from policies like the Sustainable Communities Plan (ODPM, 2003), which provides for a less rigorous planning regime in certain growth areas. These organisations can use government to skew the market in their favour, and government apparently sees little wrong with this situation because it helps to meet its objectives, while claiming it is 'working with the private sector' and using private finance. But in doing so it is binding local markets to its agenda and allowing certain organisations to benefit at the expense of others.

So we return to the demon of complexity, of things being too complex to control and manipulate consistently and over the long term. Does this mean that markets matter more than government, in the sense that we should favour market provision rather than government intervention? This is a conclusion we might readily make, but what I would rather say here is that we cannot have a combination of both: government cannot control markets and there still be freely operating markets; and government cannot use market disciplines without compromising markets and creating monopoly privileges. As Gertrude Stein[1] did not say, but might have done if she had ever written a book on housing finance: 'Government is government, and markets are markets'.

What I believe is that government ought to do what it can do, and leave markets to do what they can do. Instead of trying to introduce market disciplines into public services, it should use real markets, or if social justice or equality is its aim, then it should pursue it properly with the instruments under its control. Governments might be embarrassed about the traditional tools at their disposal, like taxing and spending, and hence they resort to the jargon of the market. But ultimately this is disingenuous, and almost certain to fail.

Markets and government action are, to an extent, opposites, and that ought to be realised, just as needs are not choices. We create conceptual distinctions for a purpose and define concepts with as much clarity and rigour as we can muster so that we can be sure what they mean and why they are important. This might appear to be an academic exercise, as an example of nitpicking, but, as Paul Shepheard (2003) stated in another context, 'a life without nitpicking is an itchy life' (p. 108). Particular politicians might proclaim a new paradigm and that choice and need can now exist together, that we can 'entrepreneur' our way to social justice (Blair, 1998) and that we can meet housing need (a statutory requirement in the UK) by using choice-based allocations systems. But this is nothing but elegant sophistry, the work of clever wordsmiths playing on the propensity of others to believe in newness and difference. As a result of this sophistry the meaning and significance of words may change, but their common usage remains; after all, that is why politicians choose them in the first place, and by a rigorous explication of the terms – of what we mean by need and choice in this case – we will get drawn back to this everyday usage. To misuse Gertrude Stein again: 'need is need and choice is choice'.

So what does this mean for housing finance? It means, I believe, that we can only seek to understand it by a clear appreciation of concepts and how they can be and are used. From this we can start to understand the place particular mechanisms – subsidies and policy instruments – can have in a given system.

What we need in order to understand housing finance is a template, a framework in which we can place the specific and particular. We need the means to locate housing finance policy. That is what this book has sought to do. In the first four chapters we have built up this template, and in chapters 5 and 6 we have sought to develop it further by looking at some mechanisms, and also by showing again in general terms how markets and government action interact, come together and conflict with each other.

There has been a bias towards developed countries, and to one in particular, but we might say the difference is in degrees, and the first four chapters of this book could be applied to developing countries with some hope of reasonable analysis being forthcoming. It might be that chapters 5 and 6 offer something of a warning for those developing countries in terms of how things might go as systems develop and government intervention becomes more extensive, and then affluence and aspiration create a change in perception about the nature of government provision.

Indeed we might argue that this book has sought to explore housing finance in conditions of relative affluence, in societies in which, to quote the Blair government in 2000, 'Most people are well housed' (DETR, 2000, p. 5). Note that not everyone is well housed, and the government did not attempt to specify a percentage or provide the numbers, so we cannot state that the problems are over. Indeed the sanguinity of 2000 looks rather ill-judged eight years later as house prices fall and first time buyers struggle to find an affordable mortgage. But still, for most people, housing is a success and so the proper emphasis is indeed on choice and aspiration; hence the importance of markets and the way they dominate even the thinking and action of government. It is as if owner occupation, as the main market-based tenure, crowds out all else and cannot permit an alternative conception of housing. For those who support markets this might be seen as no bad thing, even as they might scorn government's misuse of market concepts. But for those who see a positive role for government the reactive nature of housing policy over the last 20 years must be a cause for concern: how can housing policy have a positive impact when it can only follow in the wake of such a dominant tenure backed by an international market system? And the dominance, as it were, only becomes more prominent when that international system starts to creak and operate less well, as has been shown with the banking crisis of 2007–08.

So even when housing markets do go wrong, the government can still only react, stumbling around, not really understanding what has happened and with no real idea what is going to occur and why, but all the time claiming the opposite. Again it perhaps shows that government should steer clear of markets – not get mixed up too deeply with something it cannot understand – because, in doing so, it risks becoming entangled.

We might suggest that it is not generally good business to take over a failing bank whose share price has collapsed to the extent that it is almost worthless, in the middle of a declining market and without any idea of the eventual liabilities. Yet this is precisely what the UK government did in 2008, in the apparent belief that it could not leave the market to correct itself and just sit and watch a bank that had taken foolish decisions lose out to its competitors who had been more circumspect and market aware. Of course, this action by the UK government has not stopped other banks failing. Indeed it might have made it easier to lose money as banks know there is a precedent – what has been called, with only a little irony, 'socialism for big business' – that government will bale them out if their difficulties get too great. And nor has the market turned around as a result of government intervention. This, of course, is because the problem is not just a British one but is global. Northern Rock was borrowing funds internationally and hit difficulties when these sources dried up.

Global markets are bigger than any government, but they can still respond to the needs of individual customers. Even a government as large as the UK, even the American government, cannot control market forces. Markets have, we might say, a terrible beauty, like a storm at sea, and the actions of government in comparison are dour, colourless and timid.

Conservative thinkers, like Quinton (1993), describe politics as a tightrope. There is only a very narrow path – the tightrope – from here to there, and to get across takes skill, judgement, courage, and not a little luck. It is very easy to topple over and this can be precipitated by a lack of concentration or a sudden gust of wind. So getting across is not always a matter of things within our control, but events can intervene and cause disaster. It is, as a result, much easier for most people to fail to get across than to succeed. This is how these conservatives view government; a great deal of skill and judgement is needed, as well as an acute awareness of the risks, but events can still intervene and ruin everything. Governing is incredibly difficult and becomes infinitely more so if we attempt to carry an additional burden. We might see government's attempt to control markets as the equivalent of attempting to cross a tightrope on a windy day whilst blindfolded and carrying a wriggling baby elephant.

What we need when considering housing finance is an epistemological modesty, humility and an awareness of what we do not know. Socrates famously said that a wise person is one who knows how much they do not know. We should take this insight to heart when we consider housing finance. What we need to do is to stop before we set out on the tightrope, put down our burden and take a look at what we are attempting. We should ignore the advice that is always given at this point and actually look down, so we can see the scale of the abyss below us. And then we should take the best advice of all and draw back, go home and do something useful, something we can actually do with some safety, like count our money.

Notes

Chapter 3

1 Of course, this is limited by laws that protect the rights of others. I can use my knife but not in the same space where your chest is.
2 Of course, the effects of the credit crunch in 2007/08 have somewhat altered this position and put housing higher up the agenda. However, the response of the UK government has been to shore up the housing market, not provide more social housing.

Chapter 4

1 See chapter 5 for a fuller discussion of this issue.

Chapter 5

1 This term has come to refer to the English-speaking countries who are seen to have historic and political links, much of which has become more evident post-11 September 2001 (see Bennett, 2004).
2 A pathfinder is given funding to undertake market renewal. The idea is presumably that these schemes are breaking new ground.
3 Housing Benefit, unlike other housing activities, is non-devolved and so remains the responsibility of the UK government.

Chapter 6

1 This is being replaced by the Homes and Communities Agency in 2009.

Chapter 7

1 Stein is famous for her phrase, 'Rose is a rose is a rose is a rose, is a rose'.

Bibliography

Albon, R. and Stafford, D. (1987): *Rent Control*, London, Croom Helm.

Ball, M. (1983): *Housing and Economic Power: The Political Economy of Owner Occupation*, London, Methuen.

Barlow, J. and Duncan, S. (1994): *Success and Failure in Housing Provision*, Oxford, Pergamon.

Barry, N. (1986): *On Classical Liberalism and Libertarianism*, Basingstoke, Macmillan.

Bengtsson, B. (1995): 'Politics and Housing Markets: Four Normative Arguments', *Scandinavian Housing and Planning Research*, no. 12, pp. 123–40.

Bennett, J. (2004): *The Anglosphere Challenge: Why the English-Speaking Nations Will Lead the Way in the Twenty-First Century*, Lanham, Maryland, Rowman & Littlefield.

Blair, T. (1998): *The Third Way: New Politics for the New Century*, London, Fabian Society.

Boudreaux, K. (2008): 'Urbanisation and Informality in Africa's Housing Markets', *Economic Affairs*, vol. 28, no. 2, pp. 17–24.

Boyne, G., Farrell, C., Law, J., Powell, M. and Walker, R. (2003): *Evaluating Public Management Reforms*, Buckingham, Open University Press.

Bradshaw, J. (1972): 'The Taxonomy of Social Need', in McLachlan, G. (ed.), *Problems and Progress in Medical Care*, 7th series, Buckingham, Open University Press.

Brown, T. and King, P. (2005): 'The Power to Choose: Effective Choice and Housing Policy', *European Journal of Housing Policy*, vol. 5, no. 1, pp. 59–75.

CLG (Communities and Local Government) (2007): *Homes for the Future: More Affordable, More Sustainable*, London, The Stationery Office.

Cole, I. (2007): 'What Future for Social Housing?', *People, Place and Policy Online*, vol. 1, no. 1, pp. 3–13, online at http://extra.shu.ac.uk/ppp- online/issue_1_220507/documents/future_social_housing_england.pdf (accessed 12 May 2008).

Cole, I. and Furbey, R. (1994): *The Eclipse of Council Housing*, London, Routledge.

De Soto, H. (2000): *The Mystery of Capital: Why Capitalism Triumphs in the West and Fails Everywhere Else*, London, Black Swan.

DETR (Department of Environment, Transport and the Regions) (2000): *Quality and Choice: A Decent Home for All*, London, DETR/DSS.

DOE (Department of Environment) (1987): *Housing: The Government's Proposals*, London, HMSO.

DOE (Department of Environment) (1995): *Our Future Homes: Opportunity, Choice and Responsibility*, London, HMSO.

Doyal, L. and Gough, I. (1991): *A Theory of Human Need*, Basingstoke, Macmillan.

Dreier, P. (2006): 'Federal Housing Subsidies: Who Benefits and Why?', in Bratt, R., Stone, M. and Hartman, C. (eds), *A Right to Housing: Foundation for a New Social Agenda*, Philadelphia, Temple University Press, pp. 105–38.

DWP (Department of Work and Pensions) (2002): *Building Choice and Responsibility: A Radical Agenda for Housing Benefit*, London, Department of Work and Pensions.

Elster, J. (ed.) (1986): *Rational Choice*, Oxford, Blackwell.

Elster, J. (1999): *Strong Feelings: Emotion, Addiction and Human Behaviour*, Cambridge, Massachusetts, MIT Press.

Field, F. (1996): *Stakeholder Welfare*, London, Institute of Economic Affairs.

Forrest, R., Murie, A. and Williams, P. (1990): *Home Ownership: Differentiation and Fragmentation*, London, Hyman.

Garnett, D. and Perry, J. (2005): *Housing Finance*, 3rd edition, Coventry, CIH.

Goodin, R. (1998): 'Social Welfare as a Collective Social Responsibility', in Schmidtz, D. and Goodin, R., *Social Welfare and Individual Responsibility*, Cambridge, Cambridge University Press, pp. 97–195.

Griffin, J. (1986): *Well-Being: Its Meaning, Measurement and Moral Importance*, Oxford, Clarendon.

Harloe, M. (1995): *The People's Home: Social Rented Housing in Europe and America*, Oxford, Blackwell.

Hayek, F. (1948): *Individualism and Economic Order*, Chicago, Chicago University Press.

Hayek, F. (1960): *The Constitution of Liberty*, London, Routledge.

Hayek, F. (1967): *Studies in Philosophy, Politics and Economics*, London, Routledge.

Hayek, F. (1978): *New Studies in Philosophy, Politics, Economics and the History of Ideas*, London, Routledge.

Hayek, F. (1982): *Law, Legislation and Liberty*, London, Routledge and Kegan Paul.

Hayek, F. (1988): *The Fatal Conceit: The Errors of Socialism*, London, Routledge.

Hillier, B. (1997): *The Economics of Asymmetrical Information*, Basingstoke, Palgrave Macmillan.

Hills, J. (1991): *Unravelling Housing Finance: Subsidies, Benefits and Taxation*, Oxford, Clarendon.

Hills, J. (2007): *Ends and Means: The Future Roles of Social Housing in England*, London, London School of Economics.

Hirst, K. (2007): *Working Welfare: Welfare Recommendations for the UK Based on the US Reforms of the 1990s*, London, Adam Smith Institute.

HM Treasury (2004): *Review of Housing Supply: Securing our Future Housing Needs*, London, HMSO (also known as the Barker Report).

Irvine, A., Kemp, P. and Nice, K. (2007): *Direct Payment of Housing Benefit: What Do Claimants Think?*, York, CIH/JRF.

Jones, C. and Murie, A. (2006): *The Right to Buy: Analysis and Evaluation*, Oxford, Blackwell.

Kemp, P. (1997): *A Comparative Study of Housing Allowances*, London, HMSO.

Kemp, P. (ed.) (2007a): *Housing Allowances in Comparative Perspective*, Bristol, The Policy Press.

Kemp, P. (2007b): 'Housing Allowances in Context', in Kemp, P. *Housing Allowances in Comparative Perspective*, Bristol, The Policy Press, pp. 1–16.

Kemp. P. (2007c): 'Housing Benefit in Britain: A Troubled History and Uncertain Future' in Kemp, P., *Housing Allowances in Comparative Perspective*, Bristol, The Policy Press, pp. 105–34.

King, P. (1996): *The Limits of Housing Policy: A Philosophical Investigation*, London, Middlesex University Press.

King, P. (1998): *Housing, Individuals and the State: An Essay on the Morality of Government Intervention*, London, Routledge.

King, P. (2000): *Housing Benefit: What Government Ought to Do, but Won't*, London, Adam Smith Institute.

King, P. (2003): *A Social Philosophy of Housing*, Aldershot, Ashgate.

King, P. (2006): *Choice and the End of Social Housing*, London, Institute of Economic Affairs.

King, P. and Oxley, M. (2000): *Housing: Who Decides?* Basingstoke, Palgrave.

Koppl, R. (1994): 'Invisible Hand Explanations', in Boettke, P. (ed.), *The Elgar Companion to Austrian Economics*, Aldershot, Edward Elgar, pp. 192–6.

Levine, D. (1995): *Wealth and Freedom: An Introduction to Political Economy*, Cambridge, Cambridge University Press.

MacCormack, N. (1993): 'Constitutionalism and Democracy', in Bellamy, R. (ed.), *Theories and Concepts of Politics: An Introduction*, Manchester, Manchester University Press, pp. 124–47.

Macfarlane, A. (1978): *The Origins of English Individualism: The Family, Property and Social Transition*, Oxford, Blackwell.

Maclennan, D. (1982): *Housing Economics*, London, Longman.

Malpass, P. (1990): *Reshaping Housing Policy: Subsidies, Rents and Residualisation*, London, Routledge.

Malpass, P. (2005): *Housing and the Welfare State*, Basingstoke, Palgrave.

Malpass, P. and Aughton, H. (1999): *Housing Finance: A Basic Guide*, 5th edition, London, Shelter.

Malpass, P. and Murie, A. (1999): *Housing Policy and Practice*, 5th edition, Basingstoke, Macmillan.

Marsland, D. (1996): *Welfare or Welfare State? Contradictions and Dilemmas in Social Policy*, Basingstoke, Macmillan.

Mises, L. (1996): *Human Action: A Treatise on Economics*, 3rd revised edition, Chicago, Contemporary Books.

Mulder, C. (1996): 'Housing Choice', *Netherlands Journal of Housing and the Built Environment*, vol. 11, no. 3, pp. 209–32.

Murray, C. (1996): *Charles Murray and the Underclass: The Developing Debate*, London, Institute of Economic Affairs.

Nozick, R. (1974): *Anarchy, State and Utopia*, Oxford, Blackwell.

ODPM (Office of the Deputy Prime Minister) (2003): *Sustainable Communities: Building for the Future*, London, ODPM.

ODPM (Office of the Deputy Prime Minister) (2005): *Sustainable Communities: Homes for All: A Five Year Plan from the ODPM*, London, ODPM.

O'Neill J. (1998): *The Market: Ethics, Knowledge and Politics*, London, Routledge.

Oxley, M. (2004): *Economics, Planning and Housing*, Basingstoke, Palgrave.

Oxley, M. and Smith, J. (1996): *Housing Policy and Rented Housing in Europe*, London, Spon.

Oxley, M., Elsinga, M., Haffner, M. and van der Heijden, M. (2008): 'Competition and Social Housing in Europe', *Economic Affairs*, vol. 28, no. 2, pp. 31–6.

Page, D. (1993): *Building for Communities*, York, Joseph Rowntree Foundation.

Percy-Smith, J. (ed.) (1996): *Needs Assessment in Public Policy*, Buckingham, Open University Press.

Plant, R. (1991): *Modern Political Thought*, Oxford, Blackwell.

Popper, K. (1989): *Conjectures and Refutations: The Growth of Scientific Knowledge*, London, Routledge.

Power, A. (1987): *Property Before People: The Management of Twentieth Century Council Housing*, Hemel Hempstead, Allen & Unwin.

Power, A. (1993): *From Hovels to Highrise: State Housing in Europe since 1850*, London, Routledge.

Quinton, A. (1993): 'Conservatism', in Goodin, R. and Pettit, P. (eds), *A Companion to Contemporary Political Philosophy*, Oxford, Blackwell, pp. 244–68.

Robinson, R. (1979): *Housing Economics and Public Policy*, Basingstoke, Macmillan.

Rogers, J. (1999): 'Getting Wisconsin to Work', *Economic Affairs*, vol. 19, no. 3, pp. 28–34.

Saunders, P. (1990): *A Nation of Home Owners*, London, Allen & Unwin.

Schmidtz, D. (1998): 'Taking Responsibility', in Schmidtz, D. and Goodin, R., *Social Welfare and Individual Responsibility*, Cambridge, Cambridge Unniversity Press, pp. 1–96.

Schmidtz, D. and Goodin, R. (1998): *Social Welfare and Individual Responsibility*, Cambridge, Cambridge University Press.

Scruton, R. (2001): *The Meaning of Conservatism*, 3rd edition, Basingstoke, Palgrave.

Seldon, A. (2004): *The Virtues of Capitalism: The Collected Works of Arthur Seldon*, vol. 1, Indianapolis, Liberty Fund.

Shand, A. (1990): *Free Market Morality: The Political Economy of the Austrian School*, London, Routledge.

Shepheard, P. (2003): *Artificial Love: A Story of Machines and Architecture*, Cambridge, Massachusetts, MIT Press.

Smith, A. (1981): *An Inquiry into the Nature and Causes of the Wealth of Nations*, vol. 1, Indianapolis, Liberty Fund.

Sowell, T. (2007): *Basic Economics: A Common Sense Guide to the Economy*, 3rd edition, New York, Basic Books.

Stiglitz, J. (2002): *Principles of Microeconomics*, 3rd edition, New York, Norton.

Turner, J. (1976): *Housing by People: Towards Autonomy in Building Environments*, London, Marion Boyars.

Vallentyne, P. (2000): 'Introduction: Left-Libertarianism – A Primer', in Vallentyne, P. and Steiner, H. (eds), *Left-Libertarianism and its Critics: The Contemporary Debate*, Basingstoke, Palgrave, pp. 1–20.

Wilcox, S. (1999): *Housing Finance Review, 1999/2000*, York, Joseph Rowntree Foundation.

Wilcox, S. (2005): *UK Housing Review, 2005/2006*, Coventry, Chartered Institute of Housing/Council for Mortgage Lenders.

Wilcox, S. (2008): *UK Housing Review, 2007/2008*, Coventry, Chartered Institute of Housing/Council for Mortgage Lenders.

Wilcox, S., O'Sullivan, T. and Young, G. (2007): *Social Sector Rents in Scotland*, Edinburgh, Scottish Government.

Williams, P. (1997): 'Introduction: Directions in Housing Policy', in Williams, P. (ed.), *Directions in Housing Policy: Towards Sustainable Housing Policies for the UK*, London, Paul Chapman, pp. 1–6.

Wolff, J. (1991): *Robert Nozick: Property, Justice and the Minimal State*, Cambridge, Polity Press.